# Innovative Reflections in Pedagogy

# Innovative Reflections in Pedagogy

Dr Ismail Thamarasseri
Prof Adam Paul Patteti

GenNext Publication

*Published by*

GenNext Publication
5, Ansari Road
Daryaganj, New Delhi-110002
Phone: 011-47034999, 9811692060
E-mail: gennextpublication@hotmail.com

*Distribution Network*
gyanbooks.com
India, USA, Canada, UK, Australia, France



ISBN: 978-93-5663-463-3 (PB)

First Published, 2024

*Printed at:* Gyan Press, Delhi.



**Innovative Reflections in Pedagogy**

Author: Dr Ismail Thamarasseri, Prof Adam Paul Patteti

# Contents

# Preface

Welcome to the world of education, where the pursuit of knowledge and the nurturing of young minds have been the cornerstones of human progress. Pedagogy, the art and science of teaching, has been an essential field of study that continually evolves with the changing needs of learners and advancements in technology. In this book, "Innovative Reflections in Pedagogy," we explore into the exciting realm of educational innovation, exploring novel approaches, transformative practices, and cutting-edge strategies that have the power to revolutionize teaching and learning.

Education has always been at the forefront of societal development, shaping generations and empowering individuals to fulfil their potential. However, the landscape of education has witnessed tremendous shifts in recent times. The emergence of new technologies, the increasing interconnectedness of the world, and the demands of a rapidly evolving job market have compelled educators to reimagine their roles and adopt innovative methods to engage and educate learners effectively. "Innovative Reflections in Pedagogy" aims to provide a comprehensive and insightful exploration of these transformative changes.

The chapters within "Innovative Reflections in Pedagogy" cover a wide range of topics that encapsulate the spirit of educational innovation. Each chapter offers a unique perspective, drawing from the experiences, research, and reflections of experts in the field. Furthermore, this book delves into the power of collaboration and interdisciplinary learning, demonstrating how breaking down the traditional silos of knowledge can lead to powerful educational experiences. We explore the role of social-emotional learning, emphasizing the significance of fostering emotional intelligence, empathy, and resilience in learners. We also explore into inclusive education, discussing strategies to ensure that education is accessible to all learners, regardless of their abilities, backgrounds, or circumstances.

As you navigate through the pages of this book, you will come across a many of inspiring stories, thought-provoking research, and practical insights. Our aim is not only to inform and educate but also to inspire and ignite your own creative spark as an educator. We hope that the ideas and examples presented in this book will serve as a catalyst for your own innovative practices and encourage you to reflect on your pedagogical approaches.

As you know, the field of education is dynamic and ever-evolving, where no single approach or method fits all. "Innovative Reflections in Pedagogy" embraces this diversity and celebrates the myriad possibilities that lie within the realm of educational innovation. It encourages educators to embrace a growth mindset, continuously question existing practices, and seek new ways to engage and inspire their learners.

This book deals with the application of psychological, and sociological perspectives in educational research. Readers will acquire knowledge to integrate modern approaches in instructional practices in educational research. Additionally, the book develops the ability to critically analyse topics pertaining to gender, environment, and inclusion in educational research.

We express our heartfelt gratitude to our friends and colleagues for their unwavering emotional support and invaluable ideas, which significantly contributed to the completion of this study. Throughout the preparation of this book, we extensively referenced the works of other authors and information sources. Our deep indebtedness extends to various authors, editors, educationists, scholars, and students whose perspectives and insights have enriched the content of this book. We remain profoundly thankful to our parents, teachers, friends, colleagues, and family members for their generous guidance and assistance. Above all, we humbly seek the blessings of God Almighty and express gratitude for the strength and clarity of mind bestowed upon us to successfully accomplish this work. Finally, we extend our sincere appreciation to **GenNext Publication, New Delhi**, for graciously undertaking the publication of this book.

April, 2024

**Dr. Ismail Thamarasseri**
**Prof. Adam Paul Patteti**

# Unit - 1

# Applied Sociology

## INTRODUCTION

Applied sociology is a field of study and practice that focuses on the practical application of sociological theories, concepts, and methods to address real-world issues and problems. It involves using sociological knowledge and research to understand and analyse social phenomena, and then applying that understanding to develop strategies, policies, and interventions for social change and improvement. At its core, applied sociology seeks to bridge the gap between theoretical sociological knowledge and its practical application in various settings. It involves collaborating with individuals, groups, organizations, and communities to identify social problems, assess their impact, and propose solutions based on sociological insights. Applied sociologists may work in a wide range of areas, including but not limited to education, healthcare, criminal justice, community development, organizational management, and policy analysis. They may be employed in government agencies, non-profit organizations, research institutes, consulting firms, or academia. The goals of applied sociology are to inform decision-making, improve social conditions, and enhance the well-being of individuals and communities. It involves conducting research, collecting data, analysing social issues, and developing evidence-based recommendations. Applied sociologists often work directly with stakeholders and affected populations to better understand their needs and perspectives. Applied sociology draws on various sociological theories, research methods, and analytical frameworks to examine social structures, inequalities, social interactions, and cultural dynamics. It emphasizes the importance of considering social contexts, historical factors, and power dynamics in understanding and addressing social issues. Overall, applied sociology provides a practical and action-oriented approach to sociology, using sociological knowledge and skills to bring about positive social change and contribute to the betterment of society.

## SOCIAL CONSTRUCTIVISM

Social constructivism is a theoretical perspective in sociology and other social sciences that emphasizes the role of social interactions and cultural processes in the construction of knowledge, reality, and social structures. According to social constructivism, individuals actively participate in creating meaning and understanding through their interactions with others and their engagement with shared symbols, language, and cultural norms.

### Key Concepts of Social constructivism

- *Social Construction of Reality*: Social constructivism posits that reality is not an objective and fixed entity, but rather a product of social interactions and interpretations. It suggests that individuals collectively construct their understanding of the world through social processes, language, and shared meanings.
- *Symbolic Interactionism*: Symbolic interactionism is a central concept within social constructivism. It emphasizes how individuals create meaning through their interactions with others and interpret symbols, gestures, and language. Through these interactions, individuals develop shared understandings and negotiate the meaning of objects, events, and social phenomena.
- *Cultural and Historical Context*: Social constructivism recognizes the significance of cultural and historical contexts in shaping individual and collective knowledge. Cultural norms, values, and beliefs influence the way people interpret and construct meaning, and these interpretations change over time as societies evolve.
- *Social Construction of Knowledge*: Social constructivism challenges the idea of knowledge as a purely objective and

independent entity. Instead, it highlights that knowledge is socially constructed and influenced by cultural, social, and historical factors. Knowledge is shaped through interactions, dialogue, and negotiation among individuals and within social groups.

- *Power and Social Structures*: Social constructivism acknowledges the role of power in shaping social constructions. Power dynamics, social hierarchies, and institutional structures influence the construction of knowledge, social roles, and identities. Different groups in society may have the power to define and impose certain meanings and norms, shaping the social reality experienced by others.

## Applications of Social constructivism

Social constructivism has been applied in various areas of research and practice, including education, psychology, gender studies, and science and technology studies. In education, it emphasizes the importance of collaborative learning, active engagement, and the social context of learning. It suggests that knowledge is not transmitted passively but is co-constructed through interactions between teachers and students. In research, social constructivism informs qualitative methodologies that aim to understand the subjective experiences and meanings individuals attach to social phenomena. It encourages researchers to explore how social constructions shape people's understandings, identities, and behaviours. In summary, social constructivism provides a framework for understanding how social interactions, cultural processes, and historical contexts shape the construction of knowledge, reality, and social structures. It emphasizes the active role of individuals in shaping and interpreting their social worlds, highlighting the dynamic and socially contingent nature of human experience.

## Proponents of Social constructivism

Social constructivism has been embraced by various scholars and researchers across different disciplines. While it is difficult to provide an exhaustive list of all proponents, here are some prominent figures associated with social constructivism:

- **Lev Vygotsky**: Lev Vygotsky, a Russian psychologist and developmental theorist, is considered one of the foundational figures of social constructivism. He emphasized the role of social interactions and cultural tools in cognitive development and learning. Vygotsky's work on the zone of proximal development and scaffolding has had a significant impact on educational theory and practice.
- **Jean Piaget**: Although Piaget is often associated with cognitive constructivism, his theories also contain elements of social constructivism. Piaget emphasized that children actively construct their knowledge and understanding of the world through their interactions with the physical and social environment.
- **Peter L. Berger and Thomas Luckmann**: In their influential work "The Social Construction of Reality" (1966), Berger and Luckmann argued that reality is socially constructed through everyday interactions and shared meanings. They examined how social institutions and processes shape our perceptions of reality and the ways in which we interpret and give meaning to the world around us.
- **Kenneth Gergen**: Kenneth Gergen, an American social psychologist, has made significant contributions to social constructivist theory. He emphasizes the relational and dialogical nature of knowledge construction and argues that our sense of self and reality is continuously shaped through social interactions.
- **Erving Goffman**: Goffman, a Canadian-American sociologist, explored the role of social interactions and face-to-face encounters in his work. He examined how individuals engage in impression management and construct their identities through symbolic interaction. Goffman's work on dramaturgy and presentation of self has been influential in understanding social constructivist perspectives.
- **Bruno Latour**: Bruno Latour, a French sociologist and philosopher of science, has contributed to the field of science and technology studies with his social constructivist approach. He argues that scientific knowledge is constructed through social processes and networks of actors. Latour's

work emphasizes the social and cultural factors that shape scientific practice and knowledge production.

It's important to note that while these scholars have made significant contributions to social constructivism, there are many other researchers who have also contributed to its development and application in different fields. Social constructivism continues to be a vibrant and evolving theoretical perspective with a wide range of proponents and applications.

## SOCIAL ISSUES AND PROBLEMS

When a particular social phenomenon or condition disturbs the social order and hinders smooth working of social institutions that comes to be identified as a social problem. At the initial phase such conditions are neglected since they do not have any serious adverse effects on the social system. But gradually, they get accumulated and begin to affect normal social life. Then such condition is recognised as a social problem. Once social problem takes roots and develops beyond the bounds of tolerance, there arises resentment against it and there is a demand for remedy in the interest of social harmony. According to E. Raab and G.J. Selznick, a social problem is "a problem in human relationship which seriously threatens society itself or impedes the important aspirations of many people." In regard to the first aspect they say, "A social problem exists when organized society's ability to order relationship among people seems to be failing; when its institutions are faltering, its laws are being flouted, the transmission of its values from one generation to the next is breaking down, and the framework of expectations is being shaken". A social problem being thus defined, juvenile delinquency is to be seen "as a breakdown in society itself". The distinguished characteristic of social problems, according to Nisbet and Merton, is that "by their close connection with moral values and social institutions they from a type by themselves. They are social in the sense that they pertain to human relationship and to the normative contexts to which all human relationships exist. They are problems in the sense that they represent interruptions in the expected or desired scheme of things; violation of the right or the proper, as a society defines these qualities; dislocation in the social patterns and relationships that a society cherishes."

## Nature of Social Problems

The social problem is connected to majority of the members of society. According to Bernad, the repressive and tense condition consequent of social problems may be involving three types of elements (a) Tension factors which challenge some values of society, (b) Social values which are being challenged, (c) Intense reaction of individuals and groups to challenge. The following characteristics exhibit the nature of social problems:

- **Disintegrative:** Social problems, directly or indirectly disintegrate social system. Social problem causes dissatisfaction, suffering and misery. It seriously affects the values of the society. It is always disintegrating and disorganizing. It is pathological. It is harmful for the society.
- **Multiple Causes:** The social problems have no single or simple cause. Each problem has a complex history and is usually not due to one but too many causes. War, poverty, unemployment or crimes do not offer single or simple explanation of their occurrence. Sometimes one problem is so interwoven with other problems that it cannot be solved apart from them.
- **Inter-Connected:** Social problems are inter-connected due to which these become serious. For example, unemployment, poverty and crime are inter connected.
- **Many Remedies:** Hence the solution of the complex social problem requires various multisided remedies.
- **Relative Concept:** Social problem is relative concept. What we call a social problem in our society may not be a problem in other society. Similarly, a social problem today may not be a problem tomorrow.
- **Functional Value:** Social problem, though disintegrative, has functional value since its cure leads to social problem and social development.

## SOCIAL PROBLEMS IN INDIA

The major social problems in India are: Population problems, casteism, untouchability, regionalism, linguism and communalism, unemployment, poverty, labour problems, rural problems, problems of industrialization and urbanization, crime, suicide, juvenile delinquency, youth tensions and student unrest and finally the problems of democracy.

## Poverty

Poverty is one of the most widespread socio-economic problems of India. It is, indeed, a common problem which is being faced with most of the underdeveloped and the developing countries of the world. It is not only socio-economic but even emotional, cultural and political in nature. The developments that have been taking place in this land for the past six decades have not been able to wipe out poverty. Poverty has been the root cause of many of the problems. According to Gillin and Gillin: "Poverty is that condition in which a person either because of inadequate income or unwise expenditures, does not maintain a scale of living high enough to provide for his physical and mental efficiency and to enable him and his natural dependents to function usefully according to the standards of the society of which he is a member." According to Goddard "Poverty is insufficient supply of those things which are requisite for an individual to maintain himself and those dependent upon him in his health and vigour".

**Causes of Poverty:** The causes of poverty are many sided. However, they may be discussed under the following heads. (a) Individual incapacity, (b) Economic factors, (c) Social factors, (d) Demographic factors, and (e) Other factors. Economic causes of poverty consist Inadequate Economic Development, Increasing Unemployment, Unmanageable inflationary Pressures, Capital Deficiency and Too much Dependence on Agriculture. Social Causes consists traditionalism, illiteracy and ignorance and dominance of caste and joint families. other causes consist long period of foreign rule, climate factors, wars and threats of war, defective political system and lack of political will. Some of the major employment and anti-poverty programmes are National Rural Employment Programme, Jawahar Rozgar Yojana, and Annapurna and Antyodaya Anna Yojana.

## Over Population

Overpopulation is a major social issue in India. It is increasing very rapidly that it stands in the second position after China. Such a rise in population is a sombre aspect of the economic development of India. The population growth has led to several problems such as scarcity of food, clothes, employment and shelter, and the demands of the resources have peaked. India's population is currently increasing at the rate of 16 million each year and its annual growth rate is 1.93% as per 2001 census report. India's population is consistently increasing in all the States. Various factors have contributed to the rapid growth of population in India among which the following can be noted:

- **Excess of Birth over Death:** Growth of population depends on the excess of births over deaths. Birth rate means the number of children born per thousand of living population, and similarly, the death rate in India is very high.
- **Progress in Medical Knowledge** and its application has considerably reduced the death rate. It has helped us to control the spread of diseases like Malaria, T.B., Cholera, Plague, Influenza, Smallpox, etc., and protected the lives of people from the Jaws of death. Positively, it has contributed to greater population, because, those persons saved from the death also produced children to add to the existing numbers.
- **Improvement in Transport Facilities** has helped people to avail of medical and health facilities without much difficulty. These have saved countless lives and added to the size of the population.
- **Improvements in the field of Agriculture and Industry** also contributed to an increase in population. Uncertainties in the field of agriculture have largely been removed with the help of science and technology. Food production has considerably increased. Industries have been providing employment opportunities to thousands of persons. These developments have given people the confidence that they can afford to feed more people if they beget.
- **Certain Social Factors like Universal Marriage, Child Marriage, and Early Marriage** have also contributed to the problem. Indian consider marriage as a social obligation and almost all marriageable persons are in a married state. Life-long bachelorship is looked down upon. Particularly for women marriage is almost an inescapable obligation. Further, the number of children born per couple is also large.

- **Social Attitudes of Indians also favour an increase in population.** Poverty, illiteracy, ignorance, absence of recreational facilities, attitudes of conservatism, orthodoxy, feeling of dependence on God, a sense of resignation towards life, looking upon children as old age pension, etc..., are all responsible for the rapid growth of population.

## Unemployment

Unemployment can be defined as a state of worklessness for a person who is fit and willing to work at the current wage rate. It is a condition of involuntary and not voluntary idleness. Simply stated an unemployed person is the one who is an active member of the labour force and is seeking work, but is unable to find the same.

## Causes of Unemployment in India

Slow economic growth during the planning period the trend rate of growth was considerably lower than the targeted rate. Therefore, jobs in adequate number were not created. Further, economic growth by itself does not solve the problem of unemployment. In the recent past there has been deceleration in the growth of employment in spite of the accelerated economic growth. This can be explained in terms of steady decline in the degree of response of employment to change in output in all the major sectors of economic activity except in construction. According to T.S. Papola, over a period of time, the output growth in agriculture and manufacturing sector has become more input and technology-intensive and less labour-intensive. Besides, the sectoral composition of growth is also an important determinant of unemployment. Excessive dependence on agriculture and slow growth of non-farm activities limits employment generation.

- **Increase in Labour force:** There are two important factors that have caused an increase in the labour force which are as follows: (a) *Rapid Population Growth*: Rising population has led to the growth in the labour supply and without corresponding increase in the employment opportunities for the increasing labour force has aggravated the unemployment problem. (b) *Social Factors*: Since Independence, education among women has changed their attitude toward employment. Many of them now compete with men for jobs in the labour market. The economy has however failed to respond to these challenges and the net result is a continuous increase in unemployment backlogs.

- **Rural-Urban Migration:** The unemployment in urban area is mainly the result of substantial rural migration to urban areas. Rural areas have failed to provide subsistence living in agriculture and allied activities and so large-scale migration is taking place to cities. However, economic development in cities has failed to create enough additional jobs for the new urban entrants to the labour market. Thus, only some of the migrants are absorbed in productive activities and the rest join the reserve army of unemployed workers.
- **Inappropriate technology in India:** Despite the abundance of labour, capital intensive technology is adopted in India mainly because of rigid labour laws. It is quite difficult to follow easy hire and fire policy and so right sizing of manpower is difficult for the enterprises. It is difficult to reduce the number of labour-force. Further, the factors like labour-unrest and lack of work-culture leads to the increased inefficiency of labour and thus provide incentives to follow labour-saving technology by organizations.
- **Defective educational system:** The present educational system has theoretical bias and has limited utility for productive purposes. It lacks the emphasis on the development of aptitude and technical qualifications required for various types of work among job seekers. This has created a mismatch between the need and availability of relevant skills and training, which results in unemployment, especially of youth and educated while shortage of technical and specialized personnel continues.
- **Lack of Infrastructure Development:** Lack of investment and infrastructure development limits the growth and productive capacity of different sectors which leads to inadequate generation of employment opportunities in the economy.
- **Lack of employability:** India faces poor health and nutrition situation among masses which reduces the capacity of person to be employable and it causes unemployment.

## Casteism

Casteism is partial or one-sided loyalty in favour of a particular caste. When any mode of thinking assumes the form of an ism, it becomes rigid and partial. The sense of caste when it implies a specific status in society does not pertain to casteism. The sense of caste is converted into casteism only when consideration of superiority between castes and the tendency to consider the interest of one's own castes as opposed to the other castes are attached to it. In this manner the members of one caste do not hesitate to give fatal blows to the interests of the other castes, if the interests of their own caste are furthered in so doing. D.N. Prasad, says "Casteism is loyalty to the caste translated into politics". In this way, caste has been dragged into the political arena in the forms of casteism such as 'Brahminvada' and 'Kayasthavada'. Thus, it has been called blind group loyalty. In this all considerations of proper or improper, justice or injustice, etc, are thrown to the winds for interests of one's own caste. Casteism, therefore, is an over-riding, blind and supreme group loyalty that ignores the healthy social standards of justice, fair play, equity and universal brotherhood. According to Kaka Kalekar, "Casteism as a social problem is an over-riding, blind and supreme group loyalty that ignores the healthy social standards of justice, fair play, equity and universal brotherhood." It is clear from the above that casteism is a blind group loyalty towards one's own caste or sub-caste which doesn't care for the interests of the other castes and their members.

**Causes of casteism:** Casteism which exercises a negative influence on the network of social relations is caused by several factors of which the following may be noted.

- **Endogamous nature of the caste:** Casteism is often the result of restriction imposed on the marriage that takes place in the Hindu society. Each caste and sub-caste endogamous in nature. It means that members of a caste or sub-caste has to marry within his or her own caste or sub-caste. This practice of endogamy makes the people narrow-minded.
- **Strong desire to enhance caste prestige:** People belonging to a particular caste or sub caste have the tendency of developing loyalty to their caste or sub caste and to become more conscious of its relative prestige in society. Every

member thus tries his level best to see that his caste prestige is safe-guarded and enhanced.

- **Improvement in the means of transport and communication leading to a better organisation of caste**: Advancement that has taken place in the field of transport and communication has helped the members of the caste to be in touch with one another regularly. It has also helped them to strengthen their caste organisation and conduct activities on caste lines.
- **Urbanisation indirectly favouring casteism:** Industrialisation and urbanisation have been attracting people in a large number towards the cities. When the rural people go to the cities they naturally search for their nearer and dearer ones on the basis of the caste. They consider their own caste people as their potential friends and well-wishers.
- **Powerful hold of the caste over the members:** Caste is a strong cohesive group. It has a powerful hold over its members. Members of the caste also look to the caste to obtain the needed help and assistance in times of crises, difficulties and emergencies.

**Consequences of Casteism:** Casteism though has certain benefits to the members of the caste on the individual basis has several harmful effects on the society as a whole.

- **Hindrance to the development of national feeling**: Casteism divides people in the name of caste and encourages intolerance, jealousy, rivalry and conflicts among members of the caste. Caste clashes and tensions that arise in society for one reason or other wrecks the unity of society and damages social harmony.
- **Dangerous to democracy**: Strictly speaking, caste and democracy cannot go together. Caste is based on inequality, whereas democracy assures equality and equal opportunities to one and all. Since democracy and caste system are co-existing in India clashes between them are inevitable. Indian politics has become very much complicated because of the caste inference.
- **Encourages moral degeneration**: Casteism contributes to the moral fall. It encourages nepotism. It makes one go out of

the way to help and favour people of one's own caste.

- **Casteism leads to the negligence of talents and efficiency**: If candidates are selected and appointments are made on the basis of caste, it definitely damages talents, abilities and efficiencies of the people.
- **Casteism may even lead to Brain-Drain:** Casteism which comes in the way of the recognition of merit and efficiency indirectly promotes brain-drain.

One of the seasoned politicians of India by name Namboodiripad himself has stated "The existence of caste consciousness, caste prejudices, discontent on the basis of caste inequalities- all these are impediments in the way of the development of the country as a whole, and therefore, of the development of "lower" and "backward" castes themselves. Caste separatism, therefore, helps, the advancement of the "lower" castes themselves.

**Remedies of Casteism:** The following are some suggestions concerning the solution of the problems arising out of casteism:

- **Proper education:** The greatest need for the solution of the problem of casteism is proper education. The educational institutions should be able to provide an atmosphere in which caste distinctions are not encouraged.
- **Inter-caste marriage:** Another way of combating the continuing increase in casteism is the encouragement of inter caste marriages. Inter-caste marriage provides an opportunity for two families belonging to different castes to come together, not just two individuals, and understand each other.
- **Lesser use of the word 'caste':** One way of solving the problem of casteism is to make less frequent use of the word 'caste' so that there may be no traces of it left in the minds of the impressionable children.
- **Cultural and economic equality:** Another way of facing the problem of casteism is to introduce cultural and economic equality in the minds and the lives of the various castes.

## Alcoholism

Though alcoholism does not invariably lead to personal disorganization, it is undoubtedly an important cause of personal disorganization. In particular, the drinking habit among the poor and labour class has generated serious problems all over the world and alcoholism among poor is dangerous morally, socially and economically. The poor drink usually to escape from their besetting worries which are largely due to indigency. But as is obvious, drinking can help only to perpetuate poverty and by no stretch of imitation can be regarded as solution of this problem. Excessive drinking can help only to perpetuate poverty and by no stretch of imagination can be regarded as solution of this problem. Excessive drinking can help only perpetuate poverty and by no stretch of imagination can be regarded as solution of this problem. Excessive drinking robs a man of his sense of discrimination; he is unable to distinguish between good and bad, right and wrong. Different reasons have been given by various writers such as Caltin, Starling, Bonger and Janet, which may be summarised as; misery drinking, occupational factor, bad housing and lack of recreational facilities, ignorance, inherent nervous defects, for companionship and fun, for business reasons, urbanization, and social inadequacy.

The use of liquor and other intoxicants is harmful for every progressive and growing individual and society. It is harmful in as much as it intellectually impoverishes, morally softens and spiritually damns the person addicted to it. The harmful effects of liquor are; the wastage of national wealth, low standards of health, lowering of efficiency, mental imbalance, increase in poverty, individual disorganization, family disorganization, increase in crime, and social disorganisation.

## DRUG ADDICTION

The conditions of modern society often give scope for drug abuse. These drugs which cause serious health problems to the individuals who use it also led to some sort of dependence. Hence, they are also called "dependence-producing drugs". Though legal restrictions and prohibitions are imposed on these drugs. Though legal restrictions and prohibitions are imposed on these drugs, many individuals are found to be using them escaping the notice of the law enforcement authorities. The abusable drugs or "dependence producing drugs" belong to the following six main categories. They are: (1) Alcohol, (2) Sedatives, (3) Stimulants, (4) Narcotics, (5) Hallucinogens, and (6) Nicotine. The impact of these drugs on the individual users is not the same, but different.

- **Alcohol**: By pharmacological definition, alcohol is a drug and may be classified as a sedative, tranquilizer, hypnotic or anaesthetic, depending upon the quantity that is consumed. It relieves tension and lessens aggressive inhibitions. It includes intoxication... Alcohol has a marked effect on the central nervous system. It is not a "stimulant" as it was previously believed, but a primary and continuous depressant. Alcohol produces psychic dependence of varying degrees from mild to strong. Physical dependence develops slowly.
- **Sedatives or Depressants**: Barbiturates, bromides and tranquillizers belong to this category. These drugs are also called "drowners". They act to relax the central nervous system and induce sleep and provide a soothing effect. Medically, these are used in high blood pressure, insomnia, epilepsy and to relax patients before and during surgery.
- **Stimulants:** The most widely known stimulants are amphetamines [popularly known as 'pep-pills']. When administered by a medical practitioner, moderate dose of amphetamine can check fatigue and produce feelings of alertness and self-confidence. But the heavy dose of the same may cause extreme nervousness, irritability, head ache, sweating, diarrhoea and unclear speech. These drugs, however, do not cause physical dependence, though they are psychologically addicting. It is not advisable to take a heavy dose of it for a long time. In such cases, it may cause varying degrees of intellectual, emotional, economic and social deterioration.
- **Narcotics:** Narcotic drugs are many for they include opium, marijuana, heroin, morphine, cocaine, codeine, methadone, pithindine and cannabis such as charas, ganja, bhang etc. Continued taking of these is regarded as the worst type of addiction because it produces craving and psychic dependence.
- **Hallucinogens**: These include mescaline, DMT, STP, MDA and LSD [Lysergic acid diethylamids]. These drugs are called "psychedelics". Their use is not advised by medical practitioners. The well-known drug in this group is LSD which is a man-made chemical.

- **Nicotine or Tobacco**: This includes beedi, cigarettes, cigars, snuffs and beedi [which includes tobacco]. This leads to relaxation, stimulates and central nervous system, increases wakefulness and removes bedroom. "Tobacco is in legal use everywhere in the world, yet is causes far more, deaths than all other psychotic substances combined. About three million premature deaths a year [6% of the world total] are already attributed to tobacco smoking. Tobacco is responsible for about 30% of all cancer deaths in developed countries.

## Causes of drug addiction or motivations in drug usage

According to Ram Ahuja, the causes of drug abuse may be classified under the following four main heads: (i) Psychological factors such as – getting 'kicks' and 'thrills', relieving tension, removing inhibitions, avoiding boredom, easing depression, satisfying curiosity, feeling high and confident and intensifying perception, etc. may motivate individuals drug abuse. (ii) Physiological Factors like removing pain, getting sleep, heightening sexual experiences, staying awake, getting more physical strength etc. also induce people to become drug addicts, (iii) Social causes that favour drug abuse are – to become acceptable to friends, the desire to join "high society", facilitating social experiences, challenging social values, to set new social trends, etc., (iv) Miscellaneous Causes backing the ugly practice of drug abuse include sharpening religious insight or to get new spiritual light, improving study, solving personal problems, deepening self-understanding, increasing efficiency, to refresh the mind, and so on.

In addition to four broad categories of factors causing drug abuse, some specific may also contribute to it. Among such causes, the following ones deserve a special mention. (a) **Using Drugs for 'Kicks' or 'Thrills':** Sizeable number of street children, educated and uneducated youths become drug addicts because of their intense eagerness to taste it once. They get initiated to its use in the beginning only for 'fun' or for a 'thrill' or 'kick'. (b) **Peer Group Influence**: Peer group influence seems to be very powerful in initiating a new person to drug-taking habit. To get recognition in the company, to satisfy other members of the peer group, to feel superior in the presence of a boyfriend or girlfriend, to avoid ridicule at the hands of fellow-members-and due to such other factors young people become victims of drug abuse. (c) **Feeling of Alienation and Lack of Motivation**: The conditions of modern society are such that they may push some mentally, weak or delicate persons towards loneliness. Such persons though live in the midst of people tend to feel that they are alone in the world for they do not have any companions. (d) **To escape from the Pressure and Conflicts of Life**: Our living conditions also impose various pressures, conflicts, tensions and dangers in our life. One requires courage and a realistic approach to face such challenges of life. All are not mentally equipped to face successfully such realities of life.

**Effects of Drug Addiction:** Some of the disastrous effects of drug abuse may be noted here: Physical and Mental Decline, The Tragic Dependence on Drugs, Great Damage to Health, Moral Degradation, and Blackmailing the Drug Addicts for Criminal Purposes. Other Harmful of Drug Addiction are: (a) Drug addiction causes waste of huge amount of money on drug, (b) It damages family relations, leads to an increase in divorce, desertion and family disorganization, (c) It spoils human potentiality and prevents a large number of people from utilizing their talents and abilities for their own betterment and for the betterment of the society.

## How to Control the drug abuse/addiction

- *Educational Approach*: Imparting education about drugs and the evil effects of their consumption is of great importance. All misleading knowledge to be removed.
- *Clear Message to be given*: The message should be clear and unambiguous to the intended audience and come from credible source of information.
- *Community Approach*: The rapid changes taking place at the present time in relations between individuals, groups and nations are also reflected in a rapidly changing pattern of drug use in many parts of the world.
- *Legal Approach*: The legal control on the distribution of drugs, when effectively applied has been and remains an important approach in the prevention of drug abuse.
- *Punishment to Enforcement Agencies Including Police*: No

law or legislation is effective itself. It gets strength only if it is effectively enforced.

- *Changing the Attitudes of Doctors*: The practising doctors will have to change their approach in prescribing too many costly drugs. They have to be careful about the side effects of the drugs which they are prescribing.
- *Follow-up study of Drug Addicts under Treatment*: It is necessary to make follow-up study of drug addicts treated under detoxification programmes.
- *Role of Teachers*: Teachers can play a vital role in the prevention of drug abuse. They can talk openly and freely with the students' interests and activities.
- *Role of Parents*: Parent's role is no less significant, Drug abuse, at times, may have its roots in parental neglect, over-hostility, rejection, marital disharmony, etc. It is thus necessary that parents have to take more care in keeping the family environment congenial and harmonious.
- *Parents can do a lot in the prevention of drug abuse*: They could talk their children openly and affectionately, listen to their problems patiently and suggest them how to handle the problems effectively.
- *Providing Alternative Activities*: A popular approach to the prevention of drug abuse is providing for alternative activities which may help to prevent drug abuse.

## INCLUSIVE EDUCATION

Inclusive education is educating all students in age-appropriate general education classes in their neighbourhood schools, with high quality instruction, interventions and support so all students can be successful in the core curriculum. Inclusive schools have a collaborative and respectful school culture where students with disabilities are presumed to be competent, develop positive social relationships with peers, and are fully participating members of the school community. Inclusive education has grown from the belief that education is a basic human right and that it provides the foundation for a more just society. All learners have a right to education, regardless of their individual characteristics or difficulties. Inclusive education initiatives often have a particular focus on those groups, which, in the past, have been excluded from educational opportunities. These groups include children living in poverty, those from ethnic and linguistic minorities, girls (in some societies), children from remote areas and those with disabilities or other special educational needs. The latter are often the most marginalized both within education and in society in general. Traditionally, disabled children and those with other special educational needs have experienced exclusion, discrimination and segregation from mainstream education and their peers. Some are placed in separate classes or schools; many have been denied access to education of any sort. Inclusive education is not only concerned with disabled children, or with finding an alternative to segregated special schooling. Inclusive education encourages policy-makers and managers to look at the barriers within the education system, how they arise and how they can be removed

## Concept of Inclusive Education

Inclusion is an educational approach and philosophy that provides all students with community membership and greater opportunities for academic and social achievement. Inclusion is about making sure that each and every student feels welcome and that their unique needs and learning styles are attended to and valued. Inclusive education values diversity and the unique contributions each student brings to the classroom. In a truly inclusive setting, every child feels safe and has a sense of belonging. Students and their parents participate in setting learning goals and take part in decisions that affect them. And school staff have the training, support, flexibility, and resources to nurture, encourage, and respond to the needs of all students. Inclusive education means different and diverse students learning side by side in the same classroom. They enjoy field trips and after-school activities together. They participate in student government together. And they attend the same sports meets and plays. The concept of inclusive education evident in a variety of sources situated firmly in these key features category. These features include:

- All children attend their neighbourhood school.
- Schools and districts have a 'zero-rejection' policy when it comes to registering and teaching children in their region.
- All children are welcomed and valued.

- All children learn in regular, heterogeneous classrooms with same-age peers.
- All children follow substantively similar programs of study, with curriculum that can be adapted and modified if needed.
- Modes of instruction are varied and responsive to the needs of all.
- All children contribute to regular school and classroom learning activities and events.
- All children are supported to make friends and to be socially successful with their peers.
- Adequate resources and staff training are provided within the school and district to support inclusion.

## Points to remember

- Inclusive education (IE) is a new approach to educating the children with disability and learning difficulties with that of normal ones within the same classroom.
- It seeks to address the learning needs of all children with a specific focus on those who are vulnerable to marginalization and exclusion.
- According to Booth and Ainscow, Inclusion in education involves valuing all students and staff equally.
- It implies all learners - with or without disabilities being able to learn together through access to common schools and community educational setting with an appropriate network of support services.
- This is possible only in flexible education system that includes the needs of different types of learners and adapts itself to meet their needs.
- Inclusive education argues that all children irrespective of the nature and degree of disability should be educated in general schools with non-disabled children.
- The schools and classrooms operate on the idea that, with right amount of support, students with disabilities can be as competent as students without disabilities.

## Types of Inclusive Education

- **Partial Inclusion:** Children with disability are educated in the regular classrooms for most time of the day. For the rest of the day, they leave their regular classrooms to be with their Special education teacher aide in a resource room to work on individual academic skills or behavioural goals.
- **Full Inclusion:** A child needs to be isolated because of a skill he uniquely needs. It means that the disabled students get all the special services they need in the regular classroom and stay there all day.

## Methods of adopting Inclusive Education

- **Accommodation:** It is employed when the student is anticipated to learn similar curricular content. It is carried out when there are little changes in the services or arrangement that do not alter the learning outcomes of the students. But the student may be taught in a different way or may require some changes in the environment.
- **Modification:** It applies to student with severe disabilities. It is implemented when there are changes in the curriculum to fit the student's ability. It is usually used when a student is expected to learn a different curricular content.

## Scope of Inclusive Education

- The concept of Inclusion is often discussed as though it applies only to students with disabilities.
- In reality inclusive education has much wider scope.
- Reducing student's exclusion from schools and focusing their increase participation in the cultures, curricula and communities of local schools.
- To respond to the diversity of students in the locality, there is a need for restructuring the culture, policies and practices in schools.
- Reducing barriers to learning and participation for all students in the schools.
- Especially those who are categorized as having special educational needs.

- Acknowledging the right of students to an education in their locality. Improving schools for staff as well as for students.
- Emphasizing the role of schools in building community and developing values, as well as in increasing achievement.
- Fostering mutually sustaining relationships between schools and communities.
- The Scope of Inclusive Education on the basis of the persons it caters to can be described as ones who are covered under the title of Children with Special Needs (CWSN) as well as ones who are fully abled, yet are at a very disadvantaged position.

## CWSN includes children facing the following problems:

- Physical/Motor - Muscular dystrophy, multiple sclerosis, chronic asthma, epilepsy, etc.
- Developmental/Intellectual - Down syndrome, autism, dyslexia, processing disorders.
- Behavioural/Emotional ADD, bi-polar, oppositional defiance disorder, etc.
- Sensory Impaired - Blind, visually impaired, deaf, limited hearing etc.

## Principles of Inclusive Education

- Principle of Togetherness
- Principle of equality
- Principle of participation
- Principle of Acceptance
- Rejection of special classroom
- Individual differences
- Opposite of exclusion
- Principle of change

## Disadvantages of inclusive education

- Disabled or challenged students may not get proper help from teachers and peers which may lower down their moral.
- They may face any other problems because of inadequate facilities and teaching aids required to meet their needs.

- They may get an inferiority complex in them because of some disability.
- Gifted children may get feeling of ignorance

**Factors affecting inclusion:** The following factors are affecting the inclusion in the classroom

- **Expense**: Funding is a major constraint to the practice of inclusion. Teaching students with disabilities in general education classrooms takes specialists and additional staff to support students' needs. Coordinating services and offering individual supports to children requires additional money that many school districts do not have, particularly in a tight economy. Inadequate funding can hinder ongoing professional development that keeps both specialists and classroom teachers updated on the best practices of inclusion.
- **Mis-information**: Some of the greatest factors associated with inclusion in education are negative attitudes. As with society in general, these attitudes and stereotypes are often caused by a lack of knowledge and understanding. The attitudes and abilities of general education teachers and paraeducators in particular can be major limitations in inclusive education. Training teachers and paraeducators to understand and work with children with disabilities is often inadequate, or it may be fragmented and uncoordinated. If educators have negative attitudes toward students with special needs or have low expectations of them, children will unlikely receive a satisfactory, inclusive education.
- **Accessibility**: Obviously, a student with a disability cannot learn in an inclusive classroom if he cannot enter the room, let alone the school building. Some schools are still inaccessible to students in wheelchairs or to those other mobility aides and need elevators, ramps, paved pathways and lifts to get in and around buildings. Accessibility can go beyond passageways, stairs, and ramps to recreational areas, paved pathways, and door handles. A student with cerebral palsy, for instance, may not have the ability to grasp and turn a traditional doorknob. Classrooms must be able to accommodate a student's assistive technology devices, as well as other furniture to meet individual needs.

- **Educational modifications**: Just as the environment must be accessible to students with disabilities, the curriculum must facilitate inclusive education, too. General educators must be willing to work with inclusion specialists to make modifications and accommodations in both teaching methods and classroom and homework assignments. Teachers should be flexible in how students learn and demonstrate knowledge and understanding. Written work, for example, should be limited if a student cannot write and can accomplish the same or similar learning objective through a different method.
- **Cooperation**: One of the final factors associated with inclusion education is a lack of communication among administrators, teachers, specialists, staff, parents, and students. Open communication and coordinated planning between general education teachers and special education staff are essential for inclusion to work. Time is needed for teachers and specialists to meet and create well-constructed plans to identify and implement modifications the, accommodations, and specific goals for individual students. Collaboration must also exist among teachers, staff, and parents to meet a student's needs and facilitate learning at home.

These are just few factors that can affect students with disabilities in a general education classroom. Only a deep understanding of these factors, and other issues that hinder inclusion, and the elimination of them will make true inclusion a reality for all children to learn together

## INTEGRATED EDUCATION

Integrated education traditionally refers to the education children with special needs in mainstream settings. Disabled people of all ages and/or those learners with 'Special Educational Needs' labels being placed in mainstream education settings with some adaptations and resources, but on condition that the disabled person and/or the learner with 'Special Educational Needs' labels can fit in with pre-existing structures, attitudes and an unaltered environment. For example: the child is required to "fit in" to what already exists in the school. With the release of the Salamanca Statement in 1994 (UNESCO), a large number of developing countries started reformulating their policies to promote the inclusion of students with disabilities into mainstream schools. While a large number of developed now have policies or laws promoting "inclusive education," a number of developing countries continue to provide educational services to students with disabilities in "segregated" schools. Typically, inclusive education means "that students with disabilities are served primarily in the general education settings, under the responsibility of regular classroom teacher. When necessary and justifiable, students with disabilities may also receive some of their instruction in another setting, such as resource room". Historically, many educational systems have adopted an integrated education model as an interim approach in the move towards inclusive education. In the "integrated education" model "whenever possible, students with disabilities attend a regular school"

With the passage of The Persons with Disabilities Act in 1996, India has joined the few countries that have legislation to promote integrated education. This is a landmark step as India has now overcome a major legislative hurdle. A number of unique challenges still needs to be overcome in order to implement the key objectives enshrined in the legislation. Attitudinal barriers engrained as part of India's historical response to disability must be changed through education programmes for both teachers and the general populace. These programmes require financial and collaborative commitment from key national and state education stakeholders, and partnership with universities to support research-based initiatives. Success in achieving integrated education will ultimately depend on how Indian educators and educational systems can collaborate to deal with difference in India's culturally charged context.

**Definition:** Integrated Education is the educational programme in which exceptional children attend classes with normal children on either a part- or full-time basis. It is placement of the disabled children in ordinary schools with some specialised educational help and services. It does not necessarily integrate all the students who are away from the education for any reason like physically, mentally, socially deprived or because of any cast, creed, gender, race, ability, disability, life style etc.

**Concept:** The concept of integrated education arises as outcome of National policy of education, 1986 recommended to provide equal opportunity to all not only for access but also for success. Integration signifies the process of interaction of disabled children with normal children in the same educational setting. Integration also means 'mainstreaming' or 'Normalisation'. As disabled children are treated with normal children.

## Importance

- It does not create a feeling of differentiation among disabled children.
- It helps to remove inferiority complex among disabled children.
- It provides peer group help in learning from normal children.
- It provides disabled children a chance to enjoy school life with normal children.
- It ensures social integration.
- It inculcates affection, love and respect for differently abled children among normal children.
- It is less expensive as special infrastructure is not required. Special learning material and specially trained teachers are not appointed.
- Disabled or challenged students may get help from peers for learning and get motivated for learning

## Difference between integration and inclusion

Integrated education is similar to inclusive education but without any ideological commitment to equity. Integration places students in a mainstream classroom with "some adaptations and resources. "However, students are expected to "fit in with pre-existing structures, attitudes, and an unaltered environment." Integration is often mistaken for inclusion because students are placed in a mainstream classroom, which is a step towards inclusion. However, if there has not been a paradigm shift within the school and these students are not perceived as equals, if curriculum is not taught for the understanding of all instead of some, then the students are integrated, but not included in the school. The concept of inclusion is based on the idea that students with disabilities should not be segregated, but should be included in a classroom with their typically developing peers. A student in an inclusion classroom usually needs only to show that she is not losing out from being included in the classroom, even if she is not necessarily making any significant gains. This blanket statement does not apply to all inclusion settings, but proponents of inclusion tend to put more of an emphasis on life preparation and social skills than on the acquisition of level-appropriate academic skills.

## Special school versus integrated school, inclusive school

**Special School:** A special school is a school for children who have some kind of serious physical or mental problem. Special education is designed specifically for students with special needs, remedial education can be designed for any students, with or without special needs; the defining trait is simply that they have reached a point of under preparedness, regardless of why. Special Education is specially designed instruction, at no cost to parents, to meet the unique needs of a child with a disability. Special education is in place to provide additional services, support, programs, specialized placements or environments to ensure that all students' educational needs are provided for. Special education is provided to qualifying students at no cost to the parents. There are many students who have special learning needs and these needs are addressed through special education.

**Integrated School**: Integrated education traditionally refers to the education children with special needs in mainstream settings. Disabled people of all ages and/or those learners with 'Special Educational Needs' labels being placed in mainstream education settings with some adaptations and resources, but on condition that the disabled person and/or the learner with 'Special Educational Needs' labels can fit in with pre-existing structures, attitudes and an unaltered environment. Integrated schools educate children in an environment where self-esteem and ındependence are developed as priorities. Self-respect and respect for others are strongly encouraged. The integrated ethos is nurtured to ensure inclusion of people from different disabilities, religions, cultures, genders, abilities and socio-economic backgrounds.

**Inclusive School**: Inclusive schools recognize and respond to the diverse needs of their students, accommodating both different styles and rates of learning and ensuring quality education to all through appropriate curricula, organizational arrangements, teaching strategies, resource use and partnerships with their communities. Whilst inclusive beliefs, policies and practices specifically address the needs of students with disabilities and additional learning needs, they are equally beneficial for the full range of students. Schools that are inclusive adopt the belief that wherever possible all children should learn together regardless of differences; that all children can learn and achieve their potential; and that the continuum of students' needs should be matched by a continuum of programmes, support and services. All students regardless of their ability or disability benefit from schools adopting inclusive practices.

## HUMAN RIGHTS EDUCATION

Amnesty international defines "Though Human rights education you can empower yourself and others to develop the skills and attitudes that promote equality, dignity, and respect in your community, society and worldwide." The United Nations Declaration on Human Rights Education and Training defines human rights education as comprising "all educational, training, information, awareness-raising and learning activities aimed at promoting universal respect for and observance of all human rights and fundamental freedoms and thus contributing to, inter alia, the prevention of human rights violations and abuses by providing persons with knowledge, skills and understanding and developing their attitudes and behaviours, to empower them to contribute to the building and promotion of a universal culture of human rights." (United Nations Human Rights Council 2011). This Declaration was adopted by the UN General Assembly on Dec. 19, 2011. Human rights are part of our constitution. Every person has dignity and value. We recognize our rights and it is one of the ways every person has fundamental worth is acknowledged. There are number of basic rights that around the world and agreed it's an essential part of people. Right to life, right to fair trial, freedom from torture and other inhuman treatment, freedom of speech, freedom of religion and the right to health, education and an adequate standard of living. These are common rights for all people everywhere such as men and women, young and old, rich and poor, regardless of our background, where we live, what we think or what we believe. This makes that the human rights are universal. Human rights are a set of principles concerned with equality and fairness. They recognize our freedom to make choices about our lives and to develop our potential as human beings. They are about living a life free from fear, harassment or discrimination.

## Responsibility to protect human rights

The member states of the United Nations recognized the principle of the "responsibility to protect" in 2005 and it is called R2P. Under this principle, states have a responsibility to protect their civilian populations against genocide and other mass human rights atrocities. If they fail to do so, according to the R2P principle, states forfeit their sovereign immunity, and the international community is responsible for using appropriate diplomatic, humanitarian, and other means to protect the populations being victimized - and to this end, in accordance with the UN Charter, to be prepared to take collective action in their defence. The R2P principle was controversial because it contradicted the long-established principle of state sovereignty. It was invoked by the UN Security Council to authorize military interventions in a second civil war in Côte d'Ivoire (2010), in Libya (2011), and in other countries. However, in 2013 the international community's resistance to U.S. plans to launch missile strikes against Syria in retaliation for that country's alleged use of internationally prohibited chemical weapons against its own population added significant doubt to the already controversial assertion that the R2P principle, however warranted morally, is a legally binding principle (Weston, 2022). The following are the responsibility to protect the human rights: (1) Every individual has responsibility to protect it, (2) Government has a particular responsibility to ensure that people are able to enjoy their rights, (3) Government is the responsible authority to establish and maintain laws and services to protect t the rights.

Human rights cover effectively every area of human activity. It includes civil and political rights and Economic, social and cultural rights. The main differences of these groups are rights. In the case of civil and political rights, the government are not contradicting people access to their rights. But in the case of economic, social and cultural rights, governments must take immediate action or active steps to ensure rights being the fulfilment. These two groups of rights are briefly explained below:

- **Civil and political rights:** *Australian Human Rights Commission* refers to a person's rights to take part in the civil and political life of their community without any discrimination or oppression. It includes rights and freedoms such as the right to vote, the right to privacy, freedom of speech and freedom from torture. *The right to vote and take part in choosing a government is a civil and political right.*

- **Economic, social and cultural rights:** A person prosperity and grow and to take part in social and cultural activities. It includes rights such as right to education, health and work.

## Origin of human rights

Human rights are not a recent invention. The important of the human societies are throughout the history, ethical behaviour and human dignity. These ideas can be copied civilizations of Babylon, China and India. Laws of Greek and Roman society and Central to Buddhist, Christian, Confucian, Hindu, Islamic and Jewish teachings are the contribution of these civilization. There is also important in the concept of ethics, justice and dignity in society. It is not in written records but it consists of oral history. The ideas of justice were prominent in the thinking of philosophers in the Middle Ages, the Renaissance and the Enlightenment. Natural law was the important element of this thinking. Magna Carta (1215) was the first document that leads to some basic rights for the protection of citizens such as right to trial. It was signed by English barons the king of England. In the 17$^{th}$ and 18$^{th}$ centuries took place the idea of human rights. In 1776, American Declaration of Independence was establishing certain rights such as life, liberty and pursuit of happiness were the fundamental to all people. Similarly, in the year 1789 French Declaration of the Rights of Man and the Citizen challenged aristocracy and recognize the liberty, equality and fraternity of individuals. These values are rebounded in the year 1791 United States Bill of Rights recognized the freedom of speech, religion and the press as well as right to peaceable assembly, private property and a fair trial.

## Development of human rights

There are continues social progress are sawing in the period from 19$^{th}$ and early 20$^{th}$ centuries. Widespread extension of education, abolition of slavery and the extension of political rights are the examples. Human rights are weeks in their international activity. General attitude of a nation could not limit or liked within their boarder and other countries and the boarder international community had no basis for intervening. During this period, the term 'social sovereignty' introduced within the country has the power to rule and pass laws over territory.

Human rights are violated during the period of World War II. In 1941, US president Roosevelt proclaimed 'four freedoms' such as freedom of speech and belief, freedom from want and fear. In 1945, the war was ended but many people's lives are ruins and United Nations (1945) was the new organization help to build a better world. The observance of human rights is created one of the main aims of UN.

## Importance of human rights

Every person has self-respect and values and they are also respecting their human rights. Human rights consist set of principles and concerned with equality and justice. Our freedom makes certain choices about life and to develop our potential as human beings. We are free from fear, harassment or discrimination through our human rights. The following are the most importance of human rights.

- It can empower individuals and offer solutions for specific problems
- It is an important part of how people interact with each other's at all levels in society
- It is easy to promote justices and the well-being of society
- It enables people to claim their rights
- It teaches young people to respect diversity
- It teaches history
- It teaches people to recognize the root causes of human rights issues
- It fosters critical thinking and analytical skills
- It encourages empathy and solidarity
- It fuels social justice activities
- It helps people support organizations that uphold human rights
- It keeps governments accountable

## Principles of human rights

Human rights are inalienability and universal, interdependent and interrelated. Everyone is born with and the same rights because they are universal, irrespective of where they live, their gender, and religious, cultural or ethnic backgrounds. The principles of human rights are briefly explained below:

- **Universality and inalienability:** Human rights are universal and inalienable. In the world, everywhere, all people entitle to them. In Article 1, the university of human rights says that the universal declaration of human rights like "All human beings are born free and equal in dignity and rights."
- **Indivisibility:** It is indivisible. It is an essential part of every human person such as cultural, civil, economic, political and social issues. Therefore, all human right is equal status and it cannot be in a highest to lowest order. Every person has an adequate standard of living and it cannot compromise at any cost of rights.
- **Interdependence and interrelatedness:** It are also interdependence and interrelated. Each one contributes their own realization of a persons' human dignity and it is possible through satisfaction of their developmental, physical, psychological and spiritual needs.
- **Equality and inclusion:** All individuals are equal and by benefits of the essential dignity of every human person. There is no one to suffer the discrimination on the basis of race, colour, gender, ethnicity, age, language, sexual orientation, religion, political or other opinion, national, social or geographical origin, disability, property, birth or other status as the establishment of human rights.
- **Participation and inclusion:** All persons have right to equal opportunity to the participation in and access information related to their lives and well beings. Communities, civil society, minorities, women, young people, indigenous peoples and other identified groups are rights-based requirement of high degree of participation.
- **Accountability and rule of law:** States and the duty-bearers are the answerable persons for the observance of human

rights. They have to duty to obey or observe with the legal norms and protected international human rights instruments. They are failing in their duty; distressed rights holders are moving their rights in court or another adjudicator.

## Basic human rights

- Right to life
- Right to freedom from torture
- Right to equal treatment
- Right to privacy
- Right to asylum
- Right to marry
- Right to work
- Right to freedom of thought, opinion and expression
- Right to education
- Right to social services

## Human rights education (HRE)

The awareness of human rights is very important to understand about our rights in different situations. Human rights education is the learning that develops the knowledge, skills and values of human rights. According to United Nations Decade for Human Rights Education (1995-2004) defined human rights education as "training, dissemination, and information efforts aimed at the building of a universal culture of human rights through the imparting of knowledge and skills and the moulding of attitudes which are directed to: (a) The strengthening of respect for human rights and fundamental freedoms; (b) The full development of the developmental personality and the sense of its dignity; (c) The promotion of understanding, respect, gender equality, and friendship among all nations, indigenous peoples and racial, national, ethnic, religious and linguistic groups; (d) The enabling of all persons to participate effectively in a free society; (e) The furtherance of the activities of the United Nations for the maintenance of peace." (Plan of action of United Nations Decades for Human Rights Education 1994-2004)

Therefore, human rights education promotes values, beliefs and attitudes and encouraged all individuals to uphold their own rights and those of others. It is also having responsibility to the development of understanding of everyone's to make human rights a reality in each community. It constitutes an essential contribution to the long-term prevention of human rights abuses and represent all persons are valued and respected in s society. The fundamental rights and freedom are sets in 1998 Human Right Act. So, Human right day is celebrating December 10 in every year. Thus, Human rights education provides basis for conflict resolution and the promotion of social order. It teaches about human rights and for human rights. The main aim of this education is to help the people to understand human rights, value of human rights, responsibility to respect, protect, defending and promoting human rights. Empowerment is an important outcome.

## Aims of human rights education

The following are the some of the aims of Human Rights education

- Enhance the knowledge and understanding of human rights.
- Foster attitudes of tolerance, respect, solidarity, and responsibility.
- Develop awareness of how human rights can be translated into social and political reality.
- Develop skills for protecting human rights.
- The information about the inherent dignity of all people and their right to be treated with respect
- The information about human rights principles, such as the universality, indivisibility, and interdependence of human rights
- The information about how human rights promote participation in decision making and the peaceful resolution of conflicts
- The information about the history and continuing development of human rights
- The information about international law, like the Universal Declaration of Human Rights or the Convention on the Rights of the Child
- The information about regional, national, state, and local law that reinforces international human rights law
- The information about using human rights law to protect

human rights and to call violators to account for their actions

- The information about human rights violations such as torture, genocide, or violence against women and the social, economic, political, ethnic, and gender forces which cause them
- The information about the persons and agencies that are responsible for promoting, protecting, and respecting human rights (Nancy Flowers, Human rights educators)

Article 21-A of the Indian constitution provides free and compulsory education to all children in the age group of six to fourteen years and its aims is to be the development of human personality and strengthen respect for human rights and fundamental freedoms. Thus, the heart of human rights education is curriculum development for all stages of school education. As a guidance to develop the curriculum for children we can incorporate valuable ideas from the Vienna Declaration human rights, humanitarian law, democracy, rule of law, peace, development, and social justice. We can also add many more to provide local colour and to relate human rights with the needs of learners at different stages. Maybe some of these topics are already exist in the prevailing curriculum, but now the challenge is to make the human tights topic as the main agenda of learning. Human rights education should find its rightful place in the school curriculum, teacher training courses pre-and in-service, textbooks, supplementary reading materials, educational policies, and school administration. Human rights education must exert its influence from early childhood education onward and through a broad range of disciplines to build a human rights culture. Hence, greater commitment from all sectors and preparation of a sound, realistic plan of action can help us achieve human rights education for all and transform the human rights movement into a mass movement to achieve a better social order and peaceful coexistence. Indeed, this is one of the greatest challenges of our times. (Arshad, 2016)

## Need of human rights education

Education is human rights of everyone's. However, it is based on particular needs for a particular group, because they are weaker section of the society to facing human rights abuses, others because they hold official positions and upholding human rights is their responsibility, still others because of their ability to influence and educate. Among these groups are the following:

- Administrators of Justice viz, law enforcement personnel, including police and security forces, prison officials, lawyers, judges, and prosecutors.
- Other Government and Legislative Officials viz, members of the legislature, public officials, elected and appointed, members of the military.
- Other Professionals like educators, social workers, health professionals, journalists and media representatives.
- Organizations, associations, and groups like women's organizations, community activists and civic leaders, minority groups, members of the business community, trade unionists, indigenous peoples, religious leaders and others with a special interest in social justice issues, children and youth, students at all levels of education, refugees and displaced persons, people of all sexual orientations, poor people, whether in cities or rural areas, people with disabilities, and migrant workers (Nancy Flowers, Human Rights Educators' Network, Amnesty International USA)

## WOMEN EDUCATION AND WOMEN EMPOWERMENT

Female education is the need of the hour. Without educating the women of the country we can't hope for a developed nation. Women play vital role in the all-round progress of a country. If we want to make democracy successful, women must be educated. They are the real builders of happy homes. It is said that if we educate a man, we educate a man only, but if we educate a woman, we educate the whole family. This highlights the importance of female education. The importance of women's education is growing day by day. It is not only important to educate girls and women, but also it is necessary to provide them with basic facilities. In many countries, especially in developing countries, the literacy rate of women is low as compared to men. The main reason behind this illiteracy rate among women is the lack of proper resources. Women's education in India, the situation of women's education is not very good. According to the 2011 census, the literacy rate of Indian women was 64.6%. This number is quite low as compared to the literacy rate of men, which is 80.9%. Our society comprises men and women. In earlier times, men were considered to be the leading members of a family. They were responsible for earning the livelihood and were the decision takers of the family. On the other hand, women were responsible for doing household work and upbringing of the children. So, the roles were mainly based on gender. There was no involvement of women in decision making. If we assess our entire sector, then research says that women's issues are either focused on her reproductive role and her body or on her economic role as a worker. But none of them is focused on empowering the women. Education is necessary for the growth of any country. In India, women have traditionally been confined to household work and taking care of the family. Patriarchy is the root cause; many did not believe in educating women; instead, a female child was seen as a burden, and getting married was the only way. Another reason why families shy away from educating their daughters is the lack of safety and security. Traveling during the night and living on their own instigates fear among the families as well as the girl child. Crimes against women are on the rise, and this prevents them from receiving education. Low income forced parents to educate only the boy child, believing that he is the only breadwinner for the family while the daughter stayed at home.

The need for women's education goes back to times of independence. Savitri Phule and Jyotiba Phule were advocates for women's education and set up an institution for girls in 1848. They started the first-ever school for girls in the country in 1848 at Bhide Wada, Pune. Women were participants of the freedom struggle. The demand for women's education has been on the rise. During the time of independence, the female literacy rate was at a meagre 8.6%. According to the latest census, the female literacy rate in India is 65.5%. Though it has seen a rise, India has not met the world average of female literacy rate.

## Women Education

Women's education is essential in urban and rural areas. The education of women will help to remove the social stigma that surrounds it. It is the key to eliminating social evils such as female infanticide, dowry, child marriage, harassment, etc. This will not just help the women of today but of the future generations who can live in a world where gender equality exists. A better social status and gaining the respect of their families and peers is another reason why they must be educated. Through education, they become aware of their rights. They can contribute to the household financially and have a higher standard of living. Educating women makes them aware on taking care of their health and hygiene. Women can add to the workforce, and this contribution will reflect on the country's economy. Empowering women helps in the development of the nation. The government, over the years, has introduced many schemes to promote women's education in India. Some of the programs are; Beti Bachao Beti Padhao Yojana, Sarva Shiksha Abhiyan, Rastriya Mahila Kosh, and Mahila Shakti Kendra. The right to education is granted to every Indian citizen. We need to ensure that learning is available for all and not just for men. Spread of education in rural areas is vital as urban areas to empower women all over the country. International Literacy Day is commemorated across the globe, including India, on 8th September. The 2019 theme was 'Literacy and Multilingualism.'

## Meaning and objectives of women's education

Women's education can be regarded as a kind of knowledge given to women for enhancing their self-respect and self-dignity. This knowledge can be in form of formal, non-formal and informal education, it can also be in form of Adult Education, Community Development, Workshops, Seminars, Conferences and Training. Women's education is for making women to become economically independent and self-reliant (Bhasin, 1992), Women as mothers, are educators within their families, what they learn, they pass on to their children and their future generations (Osuata, 1987). Education for women is a development priority due to the dynamic potential of educated women. Therefore, the main objectives for women's education are as follows:

- To enable women to improve their family's health and diet.
- To increase women's productive ability, thus raising their families' standard of living.
- To give women access to appropriate technologies, management of cooperatives and the use of loan facilities.
- To improve women's social and culture status.
- To enable women to discharge their responsibilities more effectively (UNESCO, 1985).

- Helping women to fight their own fears and feelings of inadequacy or inferiority.
- Educating women in all round development. That is mentally, socially, physically, psychologically, religiously and economically.
- To make women participate fully in all the affairs of their nation and to be at centre of sustainable development.
- To make women able to acquire their own basic needs of the society, like food, shelter, fuel, clothes and nurturing.
- To enhance nation building in terms of economic and human development.

## Hindrances in women's education

In our world of today, nothing works or succeeds without education. "Today, all over the world education is the key success, to any meaningful endeavour". (Mallum, 1982) So, women need to be educated if they are to successfully contribute their quota in national development. The Blueprint on women education (1986), has identified certain problems in relations to the education of women for effective contribution to national development. These are:

- Cultural and religious factors, such as early marriages and the practice of purdah etc.
- Economic factors: such as costs of acquiring education as a tool for national development.
- School location: schools are located far away from parent's homes of the females. This brings about the problem of transportation.
- Inaccessibility of some settlement such as the riverine areas.
- Sex differentiation in occupational choice.
- Opportunity gains of formal education to parents.
- Time spent on household activities by the girls, and sometimes, girls taking care of the young ones when the mother attends school.
- The nomadic lifestyle among the Fulani tribe.
- Curriculum and instructional materials.
- Insecurity and sexual harassment from male peers or teachers.

## Why women education is important

There are Many Reasons behind why women education is important. Some of these reasons are as follows:

- Women education is important for the development of a country. A country can only develop if its women are educated.
- Educated women can play an important role in the development of their families.
- Educated women are less likely to get married at an early age.
- Educated women can contribute to the economic development of their countries.
- Women education is necessary for the empowerment of women.
- Educated women can raise awareness about various social issues.
- Educated women can act as role models for the younger generation.

## Women Empowerment

Women's empowerment can be defined to promoting women's sense of self-worth, their ability to determine their own choices, and their right to influence social change for themselves and others. It is closely aligned with female empowerment – a fundamental human right that's also key to achieving a more peaceful, prosperous world. Women Empowerment is the process that creates power in women to live a happy and respectable life in a society. Women are empowered when they are able to access opportunities in a variety of fields such as in education, profession, lifestyle, etc., without any limitations and restrictions. It includes raising their status through education, awareness, literacy and training. It also includes the authority to take decisions. When a woman makes a crucial decision, she feels empowered. Women's empowerment is the most crucial point for the overall development of a country. Suppose, in a family, there is one earning person, while in another family, both men and women are earning, then who will have a better lifestyle. The answer is simple, the family where both men and women are earning money. Thus, the country where men and women work together develops at a faster rate.

In western countries, female empowerment is often associated with specific phases of the women's rights movement in history. This movement tends to be split into three waves, the first beginning in the 19th and early 20th century where suffrage was a key feature. The second wave of the 1960s included the sexual revolution and the role of women in society. Third wave feminism is often seen as beginning in the 1990s. Women's empowerment and promoting women's rights have emerged as a part of a major global movement and is continuing to break new ground in recent years. Days like international women's empowerment day are also gaining momentum. But despite a great deal of progress, women and girls continue to face discrimination and violence in every part of the world.

## Need for women empowerment

History says that women were ill-treated. The *Sati Pratha* in the ancient times to the girl child abortion in the present scenario, women continue facing such violence. Not only this, heinous crimes against women such as rape, acid attack, dowry system, honour killing, domestic violence, etc., are still happening in India. Out of the total population, 50% of the population should consist of women. However, due to female foeticide practices, girl child numbers are decreasing sharply in India. It has also impacted the sex ratio in India. The literacy rate in girls is very low. Most of the girls are not even provided with primary education. Moreover, they are married early and made to raise children and shoulder only household work. They are not allowed to go out and are dominated by their husbands. Women are taken for granted by men as they are considered their property. Even at the workplace, women are discriminated against. They are paid less for the same work as compared to their male counterparts.

## Types of empowerments

It is evident from the above discussions that different authors and organizations have tried to define the term 'empowerment' from their own perspectives. It ranges from self-strength to efficiency building of women. However, empowerment of women now can be categorized into five main parts – social, educational, economic, political and psychological.

## Social empowerment

Social empowerment refers to the enabling force that strengthens women's social relations and their position in social structures. Social empowerment addresses the social discriminations existing in the society based on disability, race, ethnicity, religion, or gender. Empowerment as a methodology is often associated with feminism. Broadly put, the term empowerment is defined as "a multi-dimensional social process that helps people gain control over their own lives".

## Educational empowerment

"Traditional concepts recognize higher education as an instrument of personal development. It helps in growing an individual's intellectual horizons, wellbeing and potential for empowerment" (The Kurukshetra, September 2012, p. 25). It is considered as the single most important instrument of sociopolitical and economic transformation. But the picture of women's educational empowerment is not rosy in India. "The recently released United Nations Development Report 2011 ranked India 134 out of 187 countries" (The Kurukshetra, September 2012, p. 32). Without proper education to all children including girls, gender empowerment is not possible. This maxim - if one male child is literate personally, he alone becomes educated but if one girl child is educated the whole family becomes benefited - has been realized by the national political leaders, policy makers, administrators and bureaucrats. In this regard PH Sethumadhava Rao (2001) considers that, "the most important thing is that they (the women) need to be given free and compulsory education so as to make them aware of the rights and duties and possible free legal aid so that they can fight their cases without spending money." An educated mother is a one-thousand-fold superior to a mere lecturer. Education creates self-confidence, self-esteem, self-sufficiency to a person. It brings light of hope; increases social, political, intellectual, cultural and religious consciousness; broadens the length of mind; removes all kinds of bigotry, narrowness, superstition and enhances fellow-feeling, tolerance etc.

## Economic empowerment

Economic empowerment is the crying need of this hour. "Wage employment means economic power" (Elliott, 2008, p. 86). Through employment women earn money and it enables women and girls to become 'bread earners', contributing members of households with a strong sense of their own economic independence. "Economic empowerment is a powerful tool against poverty" (Biswas, 2010, p. 27). The Djakarta Declaration (1994) critically examines that, "empowerment of women is not only equal consideration; it was a necessary precondition for sustainable economic and social development." Without economic self-sufficiency other rights and scopes remain meaningless to the people. Economic empowerment can be described as a means by which the poor, landless, deprived and oppressed people of all societies can be freed from all kinds of deprivation and oppression; can directly enjoy the benefits from markets as well as household; can easily manage a square nutritious food and fulfil basic requirements such as house, cloth, medicine and pure water etc. SEWA (Self Employed Women's Association) has emphasized on the economic empowerment of women. It holds that raising voice and visibility is not possible unless there is an access "to the ownership of economic resources by the poor women." Promilla Kapur (2001) observes that, "women's empowerment could be described as a process in which women gain greater share of control over resources – material, human and intellectual like knowledge, information, ideas and financial resources like money and access to money – and control over decision making in the home, community, society and nation, and to gain power." Economic empowerment gains through equal work opportunities, equal organizational benefits, equal treatments and equal working environment.

## Political empowerment

Participation of women in the political field and in various decision-making bodies is an important tool for empowerment. The participation of women at all levels of governance structures is the highest need of this hour for women's actual empowerment. Alida Brill (2000) holds that, "Without our own voices being heard inside the government areas and halls of public policy and debate, we are without the right to accountability – a basic establishment of those who are governed." In other words, "Empowerment is not giving people power; people already have plenty of power, in the wealth of their knowledge and motivation, to do their jobs magnificently. We define empowerment as letting this power out" (Blanchard, Carlos, &

Randolph, 1996). It encourages people to gain the skills and knowledge that will allow them to overcome obstacles in life or work environment and ultimately, help them develop within themselves or in the society.

### Psychological empowerment

Through psychological empowerment women not only transgress the traditional and patriarchal taboos and social obligations, they also transform their selves and subjectivities. When women join educational institutions, political parties or decision-making bodies; hold white collar jobs, take decisions and travel different places; occupy land and wealth they feel psychologically powered and build their self-confidence, recognize their self-worth and take control of their own income and body. This joining in any institution and occupation gives them opportunities to see and to know more of the world than those who have stayed behind at home. "This personal growth and exploration have given them self-respect, pride, maturity, and resiliency as they have exerted their independence away from home". This also gives them mental strength, and makes them firm, tough and hardworking. They also learn the art of living and how to adjust with the changed circumstances. Further, it gives them satisfaction in various ways relating to work, living, learning, and adjusting in personal and financial situations.

## RIGHT TO EDUCATION

Education is critical for the holistic development of a child. It helps a child to develop different skills and behaviours which further help in developing a successful and fruitful future and an adequate standard of living. Education has a broad meaning, application and importance. It helps us with many things, but most importantly, it empowers an individual to think, question, and see beyond the obvious. Human beings are born with a natural tendency to question. Education is the best way to satisfy our curiosity, without extinguishing the burning desire to learn and explore more. Education really empowers a person to think practically and avoid illusions in the form of superstition and other religious beliefs which are really common in our country. Educated people are found to have higher self-esteem. Their lives are mostly well-planned and have a definite direction. They have better problem-solving skills and are consequently better equipped to handle everyday decisions. Hence an educated person is in a much better control of his life and also is able to give a healthier and better lifestyle for his family. Without education, life is like an empty well without water which is useful to none. Man becomes 'man' through education. Every child has the right to education. Education is a right of every individual and not a privilege. This means that the right to education is granted by law to each person. Individuals cannot be discriminated in education based on their caste, religion, sex, or economic background. In India this right is granted by the Right to Education Act (RTE), and Article 21-A of the Indian Constitution. The Right to Education serves as a building block to ensure that every child has his or her right to get a quality elementary education.

The right to education is clearly acknowledged in the United Nations Universal Declaration of Human Rights (UDHR), adopted in 1948, which states; "Everyone has the right to education. Education shall be free, at least in the elementary and fundamental stages. Elementary education shall be compulsory. Technical and professional education shall be made generally available and higher education shall be equally accessible to all on the basis of merit……" (Article 26). Apart from UDHR, right to education is affirmed, protected and promoted in numerous international human rights treaties, such as the following:

- Convention concerning Discrimination in Respect of Employment and Occupation (1958) - Article 3
- Convention against Discrimination in Education (1960)
- International Covenant on Economic, Social and Cultural Rights (1966) - Article 13
- Convention on the Elimination of All Forms of Discrimination against Women (CEDAW) (1981) –Articlc 10
- The United Nations Convention on the Rights of the Child (1989) – Article 28 and 29

The right to education has therefore long been recognized by these international treaties as encompassing not only access to educational provision, but also the obligation to eliminate discrimination at all levels of the educational system, to set minimum standards and to improve quality.

## Right to Education Act (RTE) 2009

The act is completely titled as "the Right of Children to Free and Compulsory Education Act". It was passed by the Parliament in August 2009. When the Act came into force in 2010, India became one among 135 countries where education is a fundamental right of every child.

- The 86th Constitutional Amendment (2002) inserted Article 21-A in the Indian Constitution which states: "The State shall provide free and compulsory education to all children of 6 to 14 years in such manner as the State, may by law determine."
- As per this, the right to education was made a fundamental right and removed from the list of Directive Principles of State Policy.
- The RTE is the consequential legislation envisaged under the 86th Amendment.
- The article incorporates the word "free" in its title. What it means is that no child (other than those admitted by his/her parents in a school not supported by the government) is liable to pay any kind of fee or charges or expenses which may prevent him or her from pursuing and completing elementary education.
- This Act makes it obligatory on the part of the government to ensure admission, attendance and completion of elementary education by all children falling in the age bracket six to fourteen years.
- Essentially, this Act ensures free elementary education to all children in the economically weaker sections of society.

The Right to Education Act (RTE) is important legislation that marks a watershed in the education system in India. With its enactment, the right to education has become a fundamental right in the country. The Right of Children to Free and Compulsory Education (RTE) Act, 2009, which represents the consequential legislation envisaged under Article 21-A, means that every child has a right to full-time elementary education of satisfactory and equitable quality in a formal school which satisfies certain essential norms and standards. The Article 21-A reads – "Right to education – The state shall provide free and compulsory education to all children of the age of six to fourteen years in such manner as the state may by law determine".

'Free education' means that no child, other than a child who has been admitted by his or her parents to a school which is not supported by the appropriate Government, shall be liable to pay any kind of fee or charges or expenses which may prevent him or her from pursuing and completing elementary education. The 'Compulsory education' casts an obligation on the appropriate Government and local authorities to provide and ensure admission, attendance and completion of elementary education by all children in the 6-14 ages. Private bodies are not within the Act's ambit.

## History of the Right to Education Act (RTE)

Present Act has its history in the drafting of the Indian constitution at the time of Independence but is more specific to the Constitutional Amendment that included the Article 21-A in the Indian constitution making education a fundamental right. This amendment, however, specified the need for a legislation to describe the mode of implementation of the same which necessitated the drafting of a separate Education Bill. A rough draft of the bill was composed in the year 2005. It received much opposition due to its mandatory provision to provide 25% reservation for disadvantaged children in private schools. The sub-committee of the Central Advisory Board of Education (CBSE) which prepared the draft Bill held this provision as a significant prerequisite for creating a democratic and egalitarian society. Indian Law commission had initially proposed 50% reservation for disadvantaged students in private schools. The bill was approved by the cabinet on 2nd July 2009. Rajya Sabha passed the bill on 20th July 2009 and the Lok Sabha on 4th August 2009. It received Presidential assent and was notified as law on 26th August 2009 at The Children's Right to Free and Compulsory Education Act. Thc law came into effect in the whole of India except the state of Jammu and Kashmir from 1st April 2010, the first time in the history of India a law was brought into force by a speech by the Prime Minister. In his speech, Manmohan Singh, Prime Minister of India stated that "We are committed to ensuring that all children, irrespective of gender and social category, have access to education".

- The 86th amendment to the constitution of India in 2002, provided Right to Education as a fundamental right in part-III of the Constitution.

- The same amendment inserted Article 21-A which made Right to Education a fundamental right for children between 6-14 years.
- The 86th amendment provided for a follow-up legislation for Right to Education Bill 2008 and finally Right to Education Act 2009.
- Article 21-A and the RTE Act came into effect on 1st April 2010.

## Main objective of RTE act 2009

The main objective of the RTE Act is to ensure that each child in India receives quality elementary education irrespective of their economic or caste background; this includes children who are forced to drop out of school. It also ensures that schools comply with certain regulations—regarding infrastructure and manpower—to maintain the quality of education. The Act puts the responsibility of ensuring its implementation on the government.

## Feature of Right to Education (RTE) Act, 2009

- The RTE Act aims to provide primary education to all children aged 6 to 14 years.
- It enforces education as a fundamental right (Article 21).
- The act mandates 25% reservation for disadvantaged sections of the society where disadvantaged groups include; SCs and STs, socially backward class and differently abled
- It also makes provisions for a non-admitted child to be admitted to an age-appropriate class.
- It also states that sharing of financial and other responsibilities between the central and state governments.
- It lays down the norms and standards related to; pupil teacher ratios (PTR), buildings and infrastructure, school-working days, and teacher-working hours.
- It had a clause for "no detention policy" which has been removed under the "right of children to free and compulsory education (amendment) act, 2019".
- It also provides for prohibition of deployment of teachers for non-educational work, other than decennial census, elections

to local authority, state legislatures and parliament, and disaster relief.

- It provides for the appointment of teachers with the requisite entry and academic qualifications.
- It prohibits physical punishment and mental harassment, screening procedures for admission of children, capitation fee, private tuition by teachers and running of schools without recognition.
- It focuses on making the child free of fear, trauma and anxiety through a system of child friendly and child centred learning.

## Procedure for admission under the RTE act

Children of families falling within in Economically Weaker Section category (EWS), are eligible to seek admission under the RTE Act. The EWS category includes families earning less than a certain amount of annual income. The procedure of RTE admission varies from state to state. Generally, first a school is identified in the neighbourhood. A form must be submitted along with relevant documents to prove the child's age, parents' or guardian's income, and/or caste certificate. In case of a child with special needs a certificate to prove that must be submitted. In case of a child, whose parents have died, death certificates of both parents must be submitted. Schools then screen the child based on the documents submitted to grant admission.

## The RTE Act provides for the:

- Right of children to free and compulsory education till completion of elementary education in a neighbourhood school. It is obligatory for the Government to provide free and compulsory elementary education to each and every child, in a neighbourhood school within one km, up to 8$^{th}$ class in India.
- It clarifies that 'compulsory education' means obligation of the appropriate government to provide free elementary education and ensure compulsory admission, attendance and completion of elementary education to every child in the six to fourteen age group. 'Free' means that no child shall be liable to pay any kind of fee or charges or expenses which may prevent him or her from pursuing and completing elementary education.

- It makes provisions for a non-admitted child to be admitted to an age-appropriate class.
- It specifies the duties and responsibilities of appropriate Governments, local authority and parents in providing free and compulsory education, and sharing of financial and other responsibilities between the Central and State Governments.
- It lays down the norms and standards relating inter alia to Pupil Teacher Ratios (PTRs), buildings and infrastructure, school-working days, teacher-working hours.
- It provides for rational deployment of teachers by ensuring that the specified pupil teacher ratio is maintained for each school, rather than just as an average for the State or District or Block, thus ensuring that there is no urban-rural imbalance in teacher postings. It also provides for prohibition of deployment of teachers for non-educational work, other than decennial census, elections to local authority, state legislatures and parliament, and disaster relief.
- It provides for appointment of appropriately trained teachers, i.e., teachers with the requisite entry and academic qualifications.
- It prohibits (a) physical punishment and mental harassment; (b) screening procedures for admission of children; (c) capitation fee; (d) private tuition by teachers and (e) running of schools without recognition,
- It provides for development of curriculum in consonance with the values enshrined in the Constitution, and which would ensure the all-round development of the child, building on the child's knowledge, potentiality and talent and making the child free of fear, trauma and anxiety through a system of child friendly and child centred learning.
- To Improving learning outcomes to minimise detention it introduced the Continuous Comprehensive Evaluation (CCE) system in 2009 to ensure grade appropriate learning outcomes in schools. Another reason why this system was initiated was to evaluate every aspect of the child during their time in school so that gaps could be identified and worked on well in time.
- **To Monitor compliance of RTE norms** all schools covered

under the Right to Education Act 2009 are obligated to constitute a School Management Committee comprising of a head teacher, local elected representative, parents, community members etc. The committees have been empowered to monitor the functioning of schools and to prepare school development plan.

- The Right to Education Act is justiciable and is backed by a Grievance Redressal (GR) mechanism that allows people to take action against non-compliance of provisions of the Right to Education Act 2009.
- The Right to Education Act 2009 mandates for all private schools to reserve 25 per cent of their seats for children belonging to socially disadvantaged and economically weaker sections. This provision of the Act is aimed at boosting social inclusion to provide for a more just and equal nation.

## Significance of RTE

With the passing of the Right to Education Act, India has moved to a rights-based approach towards implementing education for all. This Act casts a legal obligation on the state and central governments to execute the fundamental rights of a child (as per Article 21-A of the Constitution).

- The Act lays down specific standards for the student-teacher ratio, which is a very important concept in providing quality education.
- It also talks about providing separate toilet facilities for girls and boys, having adequate standards for classroom conditions, drinking water facilities, etc.
- The stress on avoiding the urban rural imbalance in teachers' posting is important as there is a big gap in the quality and numbers regarding education in the villages compared to the urban areas in the country.
- The Act provides for zero tolerance against the harassment and discrimination of children. The prohibition of screening procedures for admission ensures that there would be no discrimination of children on the basis of caste, religion, gender, etc.

- The Act also mandates that no kid is detained until 8th class. It introduced the Continuous Comprehensive Evaluation (CCE) system in 2009 to have grade-appropriate learning outcomes in schools.
- The Act also provides for the formation of a School Management Committee (SMC) in every school in order to promote participatory democracy and governance in all elementary schools. These committees have the authority to monitor the school's functioning and prepare developmental plans for it.
- The Act is justiciable and has a Grievance Redressal mechanism that permits people to take action when the provisions of the Act are not complied with.
- The RTE Act mandates for all private schools to reserve 25 per cent of their seats for children from socially disadvantaged and economically backward sections. This move is intended to boost social inclusion and pave the way for a more just and equal country. This provision is included in Section 12(1)(c) of the RTE Act. All schools (private, unaided, aided or special category) must reserve 25% of their seats at the entry-level for students from the Economically Weaker Sections (EWS) and disadvantaged groups. When the rough version of the Act was drafted in 2005, there was a lot of outcries in the country against this large percentage of seats being reserved for the underprivileged. However, the framers of the draft stood their ground and were able to justify the 25% reservation in private schools. This provision is a far-reaching move and perhaps the most important step in so far as *inclusive education* is concerned. This provision seeks to achieve social integration. The loss incurred by the schools as a result of this would be reimbursed by the central government.
- The Act has increased enrolment in the upper primary level (Class 6-8) between 2009 and 2016 by 19.4%.
- In rural areas, in 2016, only 3.3% of children in the 6 – 14 years bracket were out of school.

## Achievements of Right to Education Act, 2009

- The RTE Act has successfully managed to increase enrolment in the upper primary level (Class 6-8).

- Stricter infrastructure norms resulted in improved school infrastructure, especially in rural areas.
- More than 3.3 million students secured admission under 25% quota norm under RTE.
- It made education inclusive and accessible nationwide.
- Removal of "no detention policy" has brought accountability in the elementary education system.
- The Government has also launched an integrated scheme, for school education named as Samagra Shiksha Abhiyan, which subsumes the three schemes of school education: (a) Sarva Shiksha Abhiyan (SSA), (b) Rashtriya Madhyamik Shiksha Abhiyan (RMSA), (c) Centrally Sponsored Scheme on Teacher Education (CSSTE).

## Limitations of Right to Education Act, 2009

- Age group for which Right to Education is available ranges from 6-14 years of age only, which can be made more inclusive and encompassing by expanding it to 0-18 years.
- There is no focus on quality of learning, as shown by multiple ASER reports, thus RTE Act appears to be mostly input oriented.
- Five States namely Goa, Manipur, Mizoram, Sikkim and Telangana have not even issued notification regarding 25% seats for underprivileged children of society under the RTE.
- More focus is being given over statistics of RTE rather than quality of learning.

## Criticism of RTE Act

Even though the RTE Act is a step in the right direction towards the achievement of making education truly free and compulsory in India, it has met with several criticisms. Some of the criticisms are given below:

- The Act was drafted hastily without much thought or consultation being given to the quality of education imparted.
- Children below 6 years are not covered under the Act.

- Many of the schemes under the Act have been compared to the previous schemes on education such as the Sarva Shiksha Abhiyan, and have been plagued with corruption charges and inefficiency.
- At the time of admissions, many documents such as birth certificate, BPL certificate, etc. are required. This move seems to have left out orphans from being beneficiaries of the Act.
- There have been implementational hurdles in the 25% reservation of seats for EWS and others in private schools. Some of the challenges in this regard are discriminatory behaviour towards parents and difficulties experienced by students to fit in with a different socio-cultural milieu.
- Regarding the 'no detention' policy till 8$^{th}$ class, an amendment to the Act in 2019, introduced regular annual exams in 5$^{th}$ and 8$^{th}$ classes.
- In case a student fails in the annual exam, s/he is given extra training and made to appear for a re-exam. If this re-exam is not passed, the student can be detained in the class.
- This amendment was made after many states complained that without regular exams, the learning levels of children could not be evaluated effectively.
- The states which were against this amendment were six states with higher learning outcomes due to their effective implementation of the CCE system as mandated in the Act. (The six states were Andhra Pradesh, Karnataka, Kerala, Goa, Telangana and Maharashtra.)
- It has been found that many states find it difficult to move to the CCE system of assessment. This is chiefly due to a lack of teachers' training and orientation.
- Another criticism levelled against the Act is that instead of increasing the standards and outcomes of the public education system in India, it passes the buck to private schools with some respect.

Making the right to education a fundamental right took more than six decades after independence. Now, the government and all stakeholders should focus on the quality of education, and gradually move towards having a single educational system and platform across the country for all sections of society in order to foster equality, inclusion, and unity.

## NATIONAL POLICIES ON EDUCATION

The Government of India has formulated the National Policy on Education (NPE) to promote education amongst India's people. The policy covers basic education to colleges in both rural and urban India. Independent India saw a series of reforms to improve the quality and accessibility of education.

### National Policy on Education (New Education Policy) – 1968

The first-ever education policy in India was the National Policy of Education, formulated in the year 1968 which was recognized as "radical restructuring". It was promulgated by the Prime Minister, Mrs. Indira Gandhi. And was based mainly on the recommendations of the Education Commission 1964-66 (Kothari Commission). NPE 1968 was framed to equalize educational opportunities across the country. It aimed at creating an education system that can provide unrestricted access to education. This policy focused on the development of values for national integration. Because it acknowledged the power of education for the country's economic and cultural development.

**Fulfilment of the directive principle under Article 45:** According to Article 45 of the Indian constitution, there should be a provision for free and compulsory education for all children up to the age of 14 years. NPE 1968 aimed a fulfilling this directive principle. It also focused on the successful completion of the prescribed course for all enrolled students. In this way, it aimed at eliminating the barriers to quality education across all parts of the nation. The policy had the vision to create equal opportunities for citizens across the nation. Besides, it also highlighted the need to improve educational facilities for handicapped children. NPE 1968 also focused on students from rural, backward, or tribal areas. And gave special emphasis to the education of the girl child. Through this policy, the 'three-language formula' was implemented as per Article 351 of the constitution. And this encouraged the development of 'Hindi' across the country.

**Improved facilities for secondary and university level education:** The policy acknowledged the need to increase the facilities for secondary education, especially in the areas that were denied of these. It also focused on developing vocational education in order to improve employment opportunities. Under this policy, there was a special emphasis to improve the facilities in the fields like agriculture, trade, medicine, arts, crafts, commerce, home management, secretarial training, etc. Besides, it also took care in establishing new universities.

For higher-education at the university stage, correspondence and part-time courses were to be developed, similar to the online learning courses/programs that cater to students who cannot attend regular classes.

**Adult education:** To accelerate the pace of adult literacy, the policy aimed at promoting functional literacy within the masses. It targeted imparting education to the employees in the industries through literacy campaigns. And emphasized the training of the youth for improved self-employment opportunities. This policy also covered the educational interests of minorities.

**Teacher training and professional competence:** In independent India, the condition of the teachers also needed attention. The education policy in India highlighted the need to uplift the condition of teachers. And promoted their academic freedom. For their professional competence, their emoluments and service conditions were given more importance. Other than this, the policy also focused on their training and education.

**How did the NPE 1968 help in restructuring the Indian education system?** Basis the recommendations of the Education Commission, a new structure of the educational system was designed. This was the time when the country got a uniform schooling pattern in the form of 10+2+3. The visionary idea of retaining students within the mainstream education system did help in restructuring our system. Besides, it also helped in improving the overall infrastructure and educational opportunities across the nation.

**What Went Wrong?** Despite the futuristic aims of the NPE 1968, it did lack in materializing the goals of universal education for all. NPE 1968, was certainly successful in creating a structure for the nation's educational system. However, it did not succeed in bringing about the change that it was expected to. Later in the year 1986 again the next National Policy of Education was introduced in the system.

And this one was better in terms of creating a network of institutions to serve the purpose of universalization of education. NPE 1968 also suffered because of a shortage of funds. As it struggled to reach the level of expenditure which was 6% of the national income. The NPE 1968 gave a new direction to standardize education within the country. It was instrumental in creating a structure of 10+2+3 and promoted the use of the mother tongue as well.

## Key highlights of NPE 1968

- Compulsory education for all children up to the age of 14, as specified by the Constitution of India.
- Better training and qualification of teachers.
- Pay more attention on learning of regional languages, outlining the 'three language formula' to be applied in secondary education and that was: Hindi, English, and Regional Language
- Because of Hindi was adopted as the national Language the policy put wait on learning Hindi to promote it as a common language for all Indians.
- The policy also stimulated the teaching of the ancient Sanskrit language, which is an essential part of India's culture and heritage.
- The NPE of 1968 also include increase in education spending to six percent of the national income.

The next big step in the history of the Indian education system came in the year 1986 with the next education policy in India.

## NATIONAL POLICY ON EDUCATION / NEW EDUCATION POLICY - 1986

In May 1986 the new National Policy on Education (NPE) was introduce by Prime Minister Rajiv Gandhi as earlier announced in January 1985. It was named as "Special emphasis on the removal of disparities and to equalize education opportunity". The main objective of this policy is to provide equivalent opportunity for all including Women, ST and SC communities to study.

**The need and goals of NPE 1986:** This policy was formulated to improve and equalize educational opportunities within the nation. Besides, it also aimed at addressing the unique needs of the learners (including the special and marginalized students). It envisioned an educational structure that could support the all-round development of the country. And focused on the quality of education imparted within the institutions. Through a common school curriculum, the government aimed to popularize the use of educational technology. And it emphasized more on the teaching of Mathematics, Sports, Science, Physical Education and education for international understanding.

**Quality Improvement and Student Retention:** The first and foremost step under this education policy was to get all children under 14 years of age into schools. For this, it aimed at improving the school environment, student handling, and teaching methodologies. It intended a no-failure policy at the elementary school level. And also introduced arrangements for non-formal education for out-of-school students. The government opened Navodaya Vidyalayas and primary schools in remote areas. In addition, it also made arrangements for motor handicapped children either in normal schools or at district headquarters.

**Structure of Education:** As suggested by the Kothari Commission, the uniform pattern of 10+2+3 was the proposed structure for nationwide schools. This structure included 5 years of the primary stage to be followed by 3 years of the upper primary. NPE 1986 aimed to achieve the aims of free and compulsory education for all by the year 1995. And it focused on extending the schooling facility within a distance of one kilometre.

**Removal of Disparities and Special Measures:** Another important aspect of this policy was the accessibility of good quality elementary education for all. It aimed at promoting the holistic development of students through better quality schools. The policy focused on creating opportunities for non-formal education (part-time), till the time full-fledged schools were set up.

**Focus on Retention in the Mainstream System:** Most of the education policies in India considered the task of retaining students within the mainstream system. NPE 1986 too came up with an idea to shift the focus from enrolment to retention. For this, it suggested surveys (house to house) to check the regularity of attendance and relevance of schooling. It suggested creating non-formal centres (similar to the educational alternatives like online schooling) for students who are not able to attend full-day school. For regulating attendance, teachers and the members of the village education commission were expected to follow up with the families of the absentees who miss school for 2 to 3 days at a stretch.

**Provisions for the Girl Child:** Support services for girls included incentives to encourage the education of the girl child and those of the weaker sections (such as the SC's, ST's, minorities, etc.) Especially for the girl child, two sets of free uniforms, free textbooks, attendance initiatives and stationery, etc. were to be given free of cost. Apart from this, students attending elementary school were also given free transportation facilities in the state roadways buses.

**Operation Blackboard:** To ensure minimum essential facilities in primary schools the operation blackboard was launched with clear goals. It proposed the below-mentioned assistance for the schools under the operation. Two large rooms, necessary toys and games material, charts, maps, blackboards, and learning material to be provided. The resources required for the construction of buildings etc. were to be supplemented with other schemes. All in all, the policy aimed at making optimum use of the available material.

**De-linking Degrees from Jobs:** This legendary step of manpower planning created a new trend of reducing the importance of degrees from jobs. It focused on re-designing job-specific courses to help the right candidate with the required skillsets to take up a suitable job. The policy opposed undue preference to graduate candidates. Instead, it promoted the vocationalisation of education.

**How did the NPE 1986 help in restructuring the Indian education system?** NPE 1986 was amongst the most visionary education policies in India. It helped in the reorganization of education across various levels. And largely helped in streamlining a common educational structure to an extent.

**What went wrong?** Examination reforms under the NPE were not very convincing. It did talk about creating a scientific evaluation system. However, there was no concrete input to reform the general examination pattern. Despite its vision to focus on continuous evaluation, it lacked the direction to make this change within the system. In other words, we can say that it did not succeed in giving a concrete shape to some of its recommendations. And like other education policies in India, this one too suffered in implementing its recommendations because of the ongoing resource crunch. In short, NPE 1986 did aim at eliminating the disparities from the education system. However, it did not materialize its aims of standard education opportunities across various groups of the society.

**Key highlights of NPE 1986**

- Expand scholarships
- Promote adult education
- Employing more teachers from the SCs and STs Communities
- Provide incentives for poor families to send their children to school regularly.
- Develop of new institutions
- Provide housing and services.
- For primary education the NPE called "child-centred approach", then "operation blackboard" was launched to expand primary schools nationwide.
- Under this policy the Open University system was expanded with the Indira Gandhi National Open University (IGNOU), which has been created in 1985.
- The policy was also recognized as "rural university" model, based on the philosophy of Indian leader Mahatma Gandhi, to encourage economic and social development at the grassroots level in rural India.

This policy contributed to the chain of educational reforms in India. And it was again scrutinized again in the year 1992.

## REVISED NATIONAL POLICY ON EDUCATION - 1992

In 1992, the 1986 National Policy on Education was modified by the P.V. Narasimha Rao Government and later, Prime Minister Manmohan Singh has adopted it in 2005 which was recognized as "Common Minimum Programme". The National Education Policy 1986 required reformulation. A committee reviewed the NPE 1986 and came up with a detailed programme/plan of action. And the POA 1992 was framed to give suggestions in this regard.

The review committee included six education ministers, eight educationists under the chairmanship of the Chief Minister of Andhra Pradesh, Shri N Janardhana Reddy. Other than this, twenty-two taskforces including educationists and government officials were also constituted (for varied subject areas) along with a steering committee.

**The need and goals of Programme of Action (POA) 1992:** Education policies in India aim to reorganize the structure of education across different stages. Post the NPE 1986, the POA 1992 aimed at the realization of the long-term goals such as universal enrolment and retention.

**Early Childhood Care and Education:** In order to materialize the aims of the NPE 1986, the POA highlighted the need to strengthen the programs along with their components. It suggested a coordinated functioning of the government and non-government agencies to meet the goals of the ECCE programs. Under this POA, early childhood and care were given special importance. And it proposed special training (through training centres) for the Anganwadi workers to improve the quality of early childhood education.

**Universalization of Elementary Education (UEE):** Another aim of the POA was to achieve the targets for UEE. It suggested many innovations and revised schemes like the 'Non-Formal Education' for students who cannot attend full-time schools. Other than this, it also focused on 10 states (educationally backward), wherein the shared responsibility was between the centre and state government in the ratio of 50:50.

**Secondary Education:** Plan of Action 1992 acknowledged the need to further expand opportunities for secondary education. Like other education policies in India, the NPE had also envisioned better participation of the backward classes. However, the POA 1992 increased the autonomy of the Boards of Secondary Education and reorganized them. This action plan also came up with a visionary idea to improve digital literacy and technological skills in students. And this vision was helpful for the future, as in the present times we do have full-fledged online schooling and digital learning options.

**Navodaya Vidyalayas to Improve the Quality of Education:** The POA 1992 envisaged opening of Navodaya Vidyalayas across the nation. These schools were planned to help the high achievers irrespective of their socio-economic backgrounds. This proposal was quite beneficial to improve the quality of schooling for the masses. Because almost 40.7% of the students were already below the poverty line.

**Women Education:** Women education was also a top priority as per this programme of action. It suggested more development programs, and aimed at enhancing their legal literacy (about their rights). It suggested running gender and poverty sensitization programs to curb issues like gender disparity. Besides, all teachers were to be trained through innovative training programs to be the agents of women empowerment. Through institutions and women organizations, it also envisioned creating new women study centres.

**Adult Education and Micro-Planning:** Under the Non-Formal Education initiatives, the committed suggested improving the educational opportunities for adults. Innovative programs like distance education and open school system were suggested for female students residing in remote, rural, and urban areas. For students living in tribal areas, educational micro-planning was suggested. Besides, there was also a special focus on the education of adult illiterate women.

**Education for Students with Disabilities:** For 12.59 million children with disabilities, the committee suggested some important steps. To meet the needs of special students, teacher training was to be reoriented as per the inclusive classrooms. And similarly, the need to reorient non-formal and adult educational programs was also highlighted.

**How did the POA 1992 help in restructuring the Indian education system?** The Plan of Action 1992 was yet another important step towards the complex task of restricting the education system in India. Of all the previous education policies in India, this one focused the most on the development of scientific knowledge and pre-empted the need of 21$^{st}$ century schooling. It aimed at a substantial improvement within our education system. And gave attention to the aspects that can determine the progress of our developing nation.

**What went wrong?** Despite the vision of a more student-centric learning environment, POA 1992 did not suggest any concrete steps to help with this goal. It did not highlight the changes needed in the textbooks, pedagogies, and teacher training to create a more learner-centric schooling system. Even at the university level, there was no proper planning shared for resource mobilization as suggested in the POA. And once again funds mattered and these policies could not be 100% successful.

In short, it is not an easy task to make educational reforms in a country. For decades now, our policy-makers have taken some great steps to improve the condition of education in India. With NPE 1986, India got some visionary ideas to work on the core of its educational system. And the Plan of action in the year 1992 did help in modifying these as per the changing needs of the times.

## Key highlights of POA 1992

- All India basis common entrance examination for admission in all professional and technical programmes in the country.
- Under this, Government of India vide Resolution dated 18 October 200 has laid down a Three-Exam Scheme for admission to Engineering and Architecture/Planning programmes: JEE, AIEEE at the National Level, and SLEEE State Level Engineering Entrance Examinations
- State Level Institutions have option to join AIEEE
- With this problem of overlapping and also reduce physical, mental and financial burden on students on their parents which was very high due to multiplicity of entrance examinations.

## NATIONAL EDUCATION POLICY (NEP) 2020

The Union Cabinet approved the National Education Policy (NEP) in July 2020. This policy will usher in sweeping changes to the education policy of the country, including a renaming of the Ministry of Human Resource Development as the Ministry of Education. The Union Cabinet has approved the new National Education Policy 2020 with an aim to introduce several changes in the Indian education system – from the school to the college level. The NEP 2020 aims at making “India a global knowledge superpower”. The NEP 2020 cleared by the Cabinet is only the third major revamp of the framework of education in India since independence. The two earlier education policies were brought in 1968 and 1986.

**NEP 2020 Background:** The Ministry of Human Resource Development formed a committee chaired by Dr K. Kasturirangan for preparing the National Education Policy. The Committee was constituted in June 2017. The Committee submitted its report on May 31, 2019. The National Policy on Education covers elementary and university education in urban as well as rural India. NEP 2020 is the 21st Century's first education policy in India. The development of the creative potential of each student is emphasized in the National Education Policy 2020. The NEP 2020 mentioned the ancient scholars like Charaka and Susruta, Aryabhata, Bhaskaracharya, Chanakya, Madhava, Patanjali, Panini and Thiruvalluvar. The principles of National Education Policy 2020 as mentioned by the government are: Flexibility, No hard separations between subjects, curricular and extra-curricular activities, multi-disciplinary education, Conceptual understanding, Critical thinking, Ethical Values, Teachers as the heart of the learning process, and the strong public education system.

**Features of NEP 2020:** The National Education Policy as submitted by the Kasturirangan Committee submitted an education policy that seeks to address the following challenges facing the existing education system: Quality, Affordability, Equity, Access, and Accountability. The policy provides for reforms at all levels of education from school to higher education. The NEP aims to increase the focus on strengthening teacher training, reforming the existing exam system, early childhood care and restructuring the regulatory framework of education. The other intentions of the NEP include: Increasing public investment in education, setting up NEC (National Education Commission), Increasing focus on vocational and adult education, and strengthening the use of technology, etc.

## Key Recommendations of NEP 2020

**Early Childhood Care and Education (ECCE)** The NEP recommended that ECCE be developed in a two-part curriculum consisting of: Guidelines for Parents & Teachers of students up to 3 years of age and an educational framework for students between the ages of 3-8 years. The NEP talks about the implementation of these recommendations by expanding and improving the quality of the Anganwadi system and co-locating them with primary schools.

**Right to Education Act, 2009:** The NEP recommended extending the range of the Right to Education Act,2009 to include the following education levels: Early Childhood and Secondary School. This will allow coverage of RTE to all children between the ages of 3-18 years. In addition, it suggested the elimination of detention of children until class eight.

**Curriculum Framework:** Reforms in the framework of the current curriculum of school education are based on the development needs of the students. The NEP recommends the 5-3-3-4 pattern.

**School exam reforms:** Reforms in the school exam recommended by the NEP include tracking the progress of the students throughout their school experience. It includes State Census Exams in class 3, 5 and 8. Another important recommendation was the restructuring of the 10th board exam that would mainly focus and test only the skills, core concepts and higher-order thinking and capacities.

**Regulatory Structure and Accreditation of Higher Educational Institutions:** In terms of Accreditation and Regulatory structure, the NEP recommended the following changes: Setting up NHERA (National Higher Education Regulatory Authority), and Separating NAAC from UGC into an autonomous and independent body.

**National Research Foundation:** In order to improve the quality of research in India, the NEP recommended: Establishment of a National Research Foundation. It would be an autonomous body that would administer the mentoring, funding and capacity building for quality research in India.

**Education Governance:** The NEP recommended establishing an apex body for education headed by the Prime Minister under the name *Rashtriya Shiksha Aayog or National Education Commission.*

**Financing Education:** Doubling the public investment for education was one of the important recommendations of the NEP 2020. NEP 2020 insisted on the expenditure of 6% of the GDP on education. Doubling the current 10% of total public expenditure to 20% in the next decade was recommended.

**National Mission on Education through Information and Communication Technology:** The NEP suggested setting up an autonomous body that would facilitate decision making on the deployment, induction and use of technology. NEP said that this would be achieved by implementing the following measures: Establishment of National Education Technology Forum. The recommended autonomous body would be administered under this mission. It will also include virtual laboratories in various disciplines providing remote access.

**Vocational Courses:** Recommendations of NEP 2020 with respect to Vocational courses are as follows: Students in classes 9 to 12 must receive vocational education on at least one vocation, Schools should build expert curriculum delivery methods that are aligned with National Skills Qualifications Framework (NSQF) competency levels, Higher Education Institutes must also provide vocational courses that are integrated into undergraduate education programmes.

**Three Language Formula:** The Policy recommended that the three-language formula be continued and flexibility in the implementation of the formula should be provided. The three-language formula states that state governments should adopt and implement the study of a modern Indian language, preferably one of the southern languages, apart from Hindi and English in the Hindi-speaking states, and of Hindi along with the regional language and English in the non-Hindi speaking states.

**National Education Policy 2020 Concerns:** Some of the concerns expressed about the NEP 2020 are as follow:

- The report fails to address and incorporate ideas based on contemporary global thinking like the emphasis on creativity and critical thinking and the need for learning in a non-competitive and non-hierarchical ecosystem and discovering one's true passion without any sense of fear.
- Delivering the changes proposed related to Anganwadi's may be difficult despite the focus given to early childhood care and schooling.
- The propositions of volunteer teachers, peer tutoring, rationalisation of the system of schools and sharing of resources do not seem like long-term solutions.
- Lack of clarity in government strategies regarding the Public

Sector like municipal schools, state-run institutions, Kendra Vidyalaya, etc.

- The creation of a National Testing Agency (NTA) has generated scepticism. The NTA, though envisaged to serve as a premier, expert, autonomous testing organisation to conduct entrance examinations for admissions and fellowships in higher educational institutions may, in reality, lead to loss of autonomy among the universities and departments over admissions.

## Merits of New Education Policy 2020

- **Comprehensive**: NEP 2020 seeks to address the entire gamut of education from preschool to doctoral studies, and from professional degrees to vocational training.
- **ECCE**: In adopting a 5+3+3+4 model for school education starting at age 3, the NEP 2020 recognizes the primacy of the formative years from ages 3 to 8 in shaping the child's future
- **Easy on regulations:** NEP 2020 makes a bold prescription to free our schools, colleges and universities from periodic "inspections" and place them on the path of self-assessment and voluntary declaration
- **Holistic**: The policy, inter alia, aims to eliminate problems of pedagogy, structural inequities, access asymmetries and rampant commercialization.
- **Promote inclusion:** The Policy proposes the creation of 'inclusion funds' to help socially and educationally disadvantaged children pursue education

## CONSTITUTIONAL PROVISIONS ON EDUCATION IN INDIA

During 1976 Indian constitution was amended in many of its fundamental provisions. Under the Constitution of India, the Central Government has been specifically vested with several educational responsibilities. Some of the major constitutional provisions on education in India are as follows:

- **Education - both a union and a state subject:** Before the 42nd Amendment Act, education was made a state subject according to entry 11 of the List II of the Seventh Schedule to the Constitution. From 1921 to 1976, Education has been a state subject in our country under the direct control of the state education minister. But now after the 42nd Amendment Act, Education has been included in the concurrent list, and the responsibility is shared by the centre and the states.

- **Higher Education and Research:** Entries 63, 64. 65 and 66 of 'List I – Union List' dealt with various issues regarding higher education. **Entry 63** – Institutions of National Importance: "The institutions known at the commencement of this Constitution as the Banaras Hindu University, the Aligarh Muslim University and the Delhi University; the University established in pursuance of article 371E; any other institution declared by Parliament by law to be an institution of national importance." **Entry 64** – Institutions for Scientific and Technical Education: "Institutions for scientific or technical education financed by the Government of India wholly or in part and declared by Parliament by law to be institutions of national importance." **Entry 65** – Union Agencies and Institutions: "Union agencies and institutions for - a. Professional, vocational or technical training, including the training of police officers; or b. The promotion of special studies or research; or c. scientific or technical assistance in the investigation or detection of crime. **Entry 66** – Coordination and determination of standards: Co-ordination and determination of standards in institutions for higher education or research and scientific and technical institutions.
- **Free and Compulsory Education**: Being a very significant Article (Article 45) in the Directive Principles, this Article laid down the foundation of free and compulsory education in the country. Before 86th Constitutional amendment, this Article has stated that "the State shall endeavour to provide, within a period of ten years from the commencement of this Constitution, for free and compulsory education for all children until they complete the age of fourteen years". Consequent upon the insertion of Article 21 A, making elementary education a fundamental right of all children

between the age group of 6-14 years, Article 45 has been amended so as to restrict its scope to pre-primary education up to six years of age.

- **Education of Minorities**: Article 30 of the Indian Constitution relates to certain cultural and educational rights to establish and administer educational institutions. It lays down: (i) All minorities whether based on religion or language, shall have the right to establish and administer educational institutions of their choice. (ii) The state shall not, in granting aid to educational institutions, discriminate against any educational institution on the ground that it is under the management of a minority, whether based on religion or language.
- **Language Safeguards**: Article 29(1) states "Any section of the citizen, residing in the territory of India or any part there of having a distinct language, script or culture of its own, hall have the right to conserve the same." Article 350-B provides for the appointment of special officer for linguistic minorities to investigate into all matters relating to safeguards provided for linguistic minorities under the Constitution.
- **Education for weaker sections:** Article 15, 17, 46 safeguard the educational interests of the weaker sections of the Indian Community, that is, socially and educationally backward classes of citizens and scheduled castes and scheduled tribes. Article 15 states, "Nothing in this article or in clause (2) of Article 29 shall prevent the state from making any special provision for the advancement of any socially and educationally backward classes of citizens or for the scheduled castes and the scheduled tribes." Under Article 46 of the Constitution, the federal government is responsible for the economic and educational development of the Scheduled Castes and Scheduled Tribes. It states. "The state shall promote with special care the educational and economic interests of the weaker sections of the people and in particular, of the Scheduled castes and Scheduled Tribes and shall protect them from social injustice and all forms of exploitation." It is one of the Directive Principles of State Policy.
- **Secular Education:** India is a secular country. It is a nation where spirituality based on religion, had always been given

a high esteem. Under the Constitution, minorities, whether based on religion or language, are given full rights to establish educational institutions of their choice. Referring to the constitutional provisions that religious instructions given in institutions under any endowment or Trust, should not be interfered with even if such institutions are helped the State. **Article 25 (1)** of the Constitution guarantees all the citizens the right to have freedom of conscience and the right to profess, practice and propagate religion. **Article 28 (1)** states, "No religious instruction shall be provided in any educational institution if wholly maintained out of state fund." **Article 28 (2)** states, "Nothing in clause (1) shall apply to an educational institution which is administered by the State but has been established under any endowment or Trust which requires that religious instruction shall be imparted to such institution." **Article 28 (3)** states, "No person attending any educational institution by the state or receiving aid out of state funds, shall be required to take part in any religious instruction that may be imported in such institutions or to attend any religious worship that may be conducted in such institution or in any premises attached thereto unless such person or, if such person a minor, his guardian has given his consent thereto." **Article 30** states, "The state shall not, in granting aid to educational institution maintained by the State or receiving aid out of State funds, on grounds only of religion, race, caste, language or any of them."

- **Equality of Opportunity in Educational Institutions:** Article 29(1) states "No citizen shall be denied admission into any educational institution maintained by the State or receiving aid out of State funds, on grounds only of religion, race, caste, language or any of them." The Fundamental Rights of the Indian Constitution has also adopted the fourfold ideal of justice, Liberty, Equality and Fraternity. Our Constitution laid down that in the eyes of law, everyone should have an equal status, to no one the justice be denied, everyone should have liberty of thought, expression. The fundamental right of equality clearly signifies that in the eyes of law no distinction can be made on the basis of any position, caste, class or creed.

Side by side the right of equality of opportunities to all is also provided. The equality of opportunity is meaningless, unless there are equal opportunities for one's education. The well-known Kothari Commission, 1964-66 recommended that Central Government should undertake the responsibility in education for the equalization of educational opportunities with special reference to the reduction of inter-state differences and the advancement of the weaker section of the community.

- **Instruction in Mother -Tongue:** There is diversity of languages in our country. After the dawn of Independence, Mother-Tongues have received special emphasis as medium of instruction and subjects of study. In the Constitution of India, it has been laid down that the study of one's own language is a fundamental right of the citizens. Article 26 (1) states, "Any section of the citizens, residing in the territory of India or any part thereof, having a distinct language, script or culture of its own, shall have the right to converse the same." Article 350 A directs, "It shall he endeavour of every state and every local authority to provide adequate facilities for instruction in the mother-tongue at the primary stage of education to children belonging to linguistic minority groups." Secondary Education Commission, 1952-53 recommended that the mother tongue or the regional language should generally be the medium of instruction throughout secondary school stage subject to the provision that for linguistic minorities, special facilities should be made available. Kothari Commission, 1964-66 has also said that at college and university stage, mother-tongue should be the medium. The medium of instruction at school level is already mother-tongue. This is not a new proposal.
- **Promotion of Hindi:** The Indian Constitution makes provision for the development and promotion of Hindi as national language. Article 351 enjoins the Union, the duty to promote the spread of the Hindi language. Hindi accepted as the Official Language of India as laid down by the Constitution in following words: "It shall be the duty of the Union to promote the spread of the Hindi language, to develop it so that it may serve as a medium of expression of all the elements of the composite culture of India." In practice, Hindi

is already largely in use as a link language for the country. The educational system should contribute to the acceleration of this process in order to facilitate the movement of student and teacher and to strengthen national Unity.

- **Women's Education:** One of the unique features of Modem Indian Education is the tremendous advancement of Women's Education. Education of the girls is considered to be more important than that of the boys. The Constitution makes the following provisions under different articles: Article 15(1) provides that the State shall not discriminate any citizen on groups only of sex. Article 15 (3) reads: "Nothing in this article shall prevent the State from making any special provision for women and children." The well-known National Policy on Education was concerned about the status and education of women in the country. It envisages that education would be used as a strategy for achieving a basic change in the status of women. It opined that the national system of education must play a positive role in this direction. The Policy states, "Education will be used as an agent of basic change in the status of women. In order to neutralize the accumulated distortions of the past, there will be a well-conceived edge in favour of women."
- **Education in the Union Territories:** Article 239 of the Constitution states, "Save as otherwise provided by Parliament by Law, every Union Territory shall be administrator by the president acting to such extent as he thinks fit through an administrator to be appointed by him with such designation as he may specify."

## CONSTITUTIONAL PROVISIONS RELATED TO EDUCATION

Our constitution has an elaborate provision to protect the interest of the child especially for giving the right type of quality education for all. Some of the articles of the constitution are directly related to education and some others have an indirect effect on education. The articles related to education guarantees opportunities for education to all children and needy and directs the government to take the necessary steps for the national goal of education for all.

- **Article 14**. Equality before law.
- **Article 15**. Prohibition of discrimination on grounds of religion, race, caste, sex or place of birth.
- **Article 16**. Equality of Opportunity in matters of Public Employment.
- **Article 17**. Abolition of Untouchability.
- **Article 21**. Protection of life and personal liberty.
- **Article 21 A**. Right to Education "The state shall provide free and compulsory education to all children of the age of six to fourteen years, in such manner as the State may, by law, determine".
- **Article 24**. Prohibition of employment of children in factories and risky occupations. - No child below the age of 14 years shall be employed to work in any factory or mine or engaged in any other hazardous employment.
- **Article 25.** Freedom to manage religious affairs.
- **Article 28.** Freedom to attend religious instruction or religious worship in certain educational institutions. No religious instruction shall be provided in any educational institution wholly maintained out of the Stage funds.
- **Article 29**. Protection of interest of Minorities. No citizen shall be denied admission into any educational institution maintained by the state or received aid out state funds on grounds only of religion, race, caste, language or any of them.
- **Article 30**. Right of minorities to establish and administer educational institutions of their choice.
- **Article 45**. "The state shall endeavour to provide early childhood care and education for all children until they complete the age of six years."
- **Article 46**. Promotion of educational and economic interests of Scheduled Castes, Scheduled Tribes and other weaker sections. "The state shall promote with special care, the educational and economic interests of the weaker sections of the people, and, in particular, of the Scheduled Castes and the Scheduled Tribes, and shall protect them from social injustice and all forms of exploitation".

- **Article 51 A (k).** "Who is a parent or guardian to provide opportunities for education to his child or as the case may be, ward between the age of six and fourteen years." It stresses the responsibility of the parent in providing educational opportunities to his child.
- **Article 337**. Special provision with respect to educational grants for the benefit of Anglo-Indian community.
- **Article 338**. It makes provision for the appointment of a special officer for Scheduled Castes and Scheduled Tribes.
- **Article 340**. It envisages the appointment of the commission to investigate the conditions of the backward classes.
- **Article 350 A.** Facilities for instruction in Mother-tongue at primary stage.

In short, Education has always remained a key area of concern for both nation builders and policy makers. When the Constitution of India was written and adopted, due weightage was given to ensure opportunities for education to all. Equality and equity were the core values behind all provisions. Here we discussed about Right to Education, National Polices on Education and all major articles and amendments related to education of the Constitution of India which are having educational relevance. In 2002, through 86$^{th}$ constitutional amendment, education became fundamental right of Indian citizens. The enactment of Right to Education Act, 2009 was a great turning point to implement it. Educational policy is important because it keeps all institutions within the framework of the law and forces them to abide by it, failing to do so resulting in penalties prescribed in the policy. The Indian constitution requires the government to promote the educational interests of the socially, culturally, and economically disadvantaged sections of society. There are many provisions made in our constitutions for the upliftment of weaker sections of our society, all these have been discussed in brief in the above sessions.

## CONCLUSION

These social issues prevent the path of India towards development. However, with the changing time, there is an increase in the awareness among the common people, which will solely curb these ailments of social issues from the country. So, both the government and the commoner should walk hand in hand to tackle the current social issues in India. Rights are legal, social or ethical principles of freedom of entitlement and these are based on legal system. It is also important in disciplines as law and ethics especially for theories of justice and deontology. However, human rights education is an essential part of our life and also responsible person to protect it. It is the learning that develops our knowledge, skills and value of human rights. Hence, human rights education is an important part in our educational system. It is not only in the school level but also in our university curriculum. Every human being has the rights and freedoms to understand through the teaching of basic principle of non-discrimination and the fundamental rights and freedoms. Women education is very important for the development of a country. It is necessary to provide girls and women with proper resources so that they can get educated. Girls and women have the potential to contribute to the economic development of their countries. They can also play an important role in the development of their families. Therefore, it is necessary to pay more attention to women education. It is now well-known fact that the issue of women's empowerment for the positive change and transformation of the existing unequal society is more crucial and more important. So far women's role as mothers, homemakers, wives and sisters are well known, but their role in shifting the entire power relations of a country is a modern concept.

## REFERENCES


1. Antony, V. (2006). Education and employment: The key to women's empowerment. *Kurukshetra*, Ministry of Rural Development, New Delhi.
2. Arshad, M. S. (2016). *Why it is important to include Human Rights Education in School Curriculum of Children.* Linkedin.com
3. Aspy, C. B., & Sandhu, D. S. (1999). *Empowering women for equity: A counselling approach.* American Counselling Association, Alexandria
4. Batliwala, S. (1995). Meaning of women's empowerment. *Women's World*, 23-34
5. Bhatnagar, S. & Gill, S. (2014). Right to Education: Comparative Analysis of different countries. *Journal of Research in Humanities and Social Science*, *2*(2), 29-32.
6. Biswas, S.K. (2010). New Tribal Panchayat in Nicobar Islands. *Kurukshetra*, Ministry of Rural Development, New Delhi
7. Brown & Margot. (1996). *Our World, Our Rights: Teaching about Rights &*

*Responsibilities in the Elementary School*. London: Amnesty International UK and Education in Human Rights Network,

8. Claude & Pierre, R. (1997). *Methodologies for Human Rights Education*. New York, NY: Peoples Decade for Human Rights Education.
9. *Constitutional Provisions on Education in India,* retrieved from https://physicscatalyst.com.
10. Flowers, N. *Human Rights Educators' Network*, Amnesty International USA
11. Gazette of India Extraordinary Part II *The right of children to free and compulsory education act, 2009*. Retrieved from https://www.education.gov.in › mhrd.
12. Government of India. (1995). *Country Report: Development of women and child*. Ministry of Human Resource Development. Fourth World Conference on Women, Beijing.
13. Henry &Kenneth. (1978). *Social Problems: Institutional and Interpersonal Perspectives*, Scott, Fopresman and Company, Illinois, London
14. http://hrlibrary.umn.edu/edumat/hreduseries/hereandnow/Part-2/HRE-intro.htm
15. https://en.unesco.org/news/what-you-need-know-about-right-education
16. https://en.wikipedia.org/wiki/Human_rights_education
17. https://sur.conectas.org/en/right-education-human-rights-education/
18. https://www.hrw.org/students-and-educators
19. https://www.socialstudies.org/position-statements/human-rights-education
20. Khan, Z. (2020). *12 Major Constitutional Provisions on Education in India,* retrieved from https://www.yourarticlelibrary.com.
21. Merton, R.K. & Nisbet, R. (1976). *Contemporary Social Problems*, Hercourt Brace Iovanovich, International Editing, New York, Chicago.
22. Narasimhan, S. (1999). *Empowering women: An alternative strategy from rural India*. Sage, New Delhi.
23. *National Education Policy 2020* Retrieved from https://www.education.gov.in.
24. NCERT. (1987). *Project Integrated Education for the Disabled (PIED)*. New Delhi: National Council of Educational Research and Training.
25. Paul, M, J. (1996). *Self-Help Human Rights Education Handbook*. New York, NY: Center for the Study of Human Rights, Columbia University.
26. Ram, A. (1992). *Social Problems in India*, Rawat Publications, New Delhi.
27. Rehabilitation Council of India. (1996). *Report on Manpower Development*. New Delhi: Ministry of Welfare, Govt. of India.
28. *Right of Children to Free and Compulsory Education Act, 2009 (Right to Education Act)* Retrieved from http://vikaspedia.in.

29. Sharma, K. (1992). *Integrating children with special needs*. Agra: National psychological Corporation.

30. Sharma, U., & Desai, I. (2002). Measuring concerns about integrated education in India. *Asia and Pacific Journal on Disability,* 5(1), 2-14.

31. Shiman, D. (1999). *Teaching Human Rights*. Denver, CO: Centre for Teaching International Relations.

32. Singh, G. (2012). Importance of education in the changing scenario. *Kurukshetra*, September, Ministry of Rural Development, New Delhi.

33. Tamang, A. (2012). The challenge of ensuring equal access to education for women: A critical analysis. *Kurukshetra*, 60(11). New Delhi.

34. Thankachan, T.C. (2007). *Philosophical and Sociological Bases of Education*. Kottayam: V Publishers.

35. Turner, J.H. (1987). *The Structure of Sociological Theory*, Rawat Publications, Jaipur.

36. UNESCO. *Salamanca Statement, 1994.* Retrieved November 17, 2004, from https://www.unesco.org/en

37. Walia, J.S. (1998). *Foundations of Education*. Punjab: Paul Publishers.

38. http://portal.unesco.org/education/en

39. WHO (1980). *International classification of impairments, disabilities, and handicaps.* Geneva: WHO.

40. Yadav, A. (2019). *Right to Free and Compulsory Education,* retrieved from https://blog.ipleaders.in.

# Unit - 2

# Modern Instructional Approaches

## Introduction

In the ever-evolving domain of education, the integration of modern instructional approaches has become paramount to cater to the diverse needs of learners and to harness the potential of emerging technologies. This chapter delves into a comprehensive exploration of various contemporary methodologies and tools that educators employ to enhance the teaching and learning experience. From leveraging the power of technology to facilitate learning anytime and anywhere, to employing innovative pedagogical frameworks and assessment strategies, this chapter illuminates the dynamic intersection of theory and practice in modern education.

We begin by examining the transformative impact of technology-enhanced learning (TEL) and cloud computing on educational paradigms. TEL has revolutionized the traditional classroom setting by providing learners with access to a myriad of digital resources, collaborative platforms, and personalized learning experiences. Concurrently, cloud computing has facilitated the seamless storage, retrieval, and sharing of educational content, fostering greater flexibility and scalability in educational delivery. Furthermore, the proliferation of mobile devices has spurred the emergence of mobile learning (M-learning) and ubiquitous learning (U-learning), enabling learners to engage with educational content beyond the confines of traditional learning environments. These mobile-centric approaches empower learners to take ownership of their learning journey while promoting continuous engagement and interaction.

Moreover, we delve into the significance of conceptual and mind mapping as cognitive tools for organizing and synthesizing information, fostering critical thinking skills, and enhancing knowledge retention. Through exploring models of teaching and curriculum development, we elucidate the diverse pedagogical frameworks and strategies that educators employ to facilitate effective learning experiences tailored to the needs of their learners. Additionally, this chapter elucidates the relevance of seminal frameworks such as Bloom's Taxonomy in informing instructional design and assessment practices, guiding educators in the formulation of learning objectives and the evaluation of learning outcomes. Furthermore, we examine the role of standardized achievement tests in gauging learner proficiency and informing instructional decision-making. Finally, we explore prominent instructional design models such as Laurillard's conversational model and the Five Stage Model of Gilly Salmon, elucidating their application in designing engaging and interactive learning experiences that foster collaboration, reflection, and knowledge construction. By navigating through the multifaceted terrain of modern instructional approaches, this chapter endeavours to equip educators with the requisite knowledge and tools to navigate the complexities of contemporary education and empower learners to thrive in the digital age.

## TECHNOLOGY ENHANCED LEARNING (TEL)

Learning has been influenced by technology at least since pre-historic period. Technology is changing day by day. Now the technology is based on digital systems. Digital technology is highly interactive. Computers and more recently mobile devices can not only provide teaching materials through a variety of media, they can also respond to learners by linking between webpages reacting to queries and engaging in games and simulations. Technology Enhanced Learning (TEL) harnesses the power of interactivity and has the potential to enhance what is learned, how we learn and what we teach.

### Digital Era

Early man used tools for life itself, developed things like stick, stone, bone, charcoal for writing, painting, carving, sculpture etc. Later printing, handicraft, electric machines etc were popularised. Before the digital era different technologies were used in the early period. Instructional film, Pressy's teaching machine, instructional radio, instructional television, audio cassette, video cassette and microcomputer were used in teaching learning process. The latest developments in science and technology have a lot of applications in education. The term Technology-enhanced learning (TEL) is used to describe the application of technology to teaching and learning. It is a broad category that isn't particularly defined, but it is transforming education and educational institutions beyond recognition.

## Why TEL is important?

- **Quick changes in technology:** The domain of education is confronted with great challenge to improve its practice of learning and teaching, to improve its research efforts and to achieve valuable innovations. Now new technologies are flooding the markets and learners, be it school children or adult professionals, except high quality, flexible, modern, and tailored services.
- **The internet as a social revolution:** The emergence of the internet in the 1990's marks a fundamental change of the way society functions. The all-embracing nature of the internet produced a new conceptualisation of information access, information service and social connectedness. By enabling the self-evident access to an abundance of information, it promotes liberal, democratic values and the independent, self-directed, responsible citizens that represent these. The all-embracing nature of the internet has amplified the global economy and exchange of cultures. The values of openness and self-directedness are more and more adopted in today's boundaries between the school building and outside society. Also, the internet the first technological innovation that enables education providers to implement changes at an institution, organisational level. This way the microcomputer transformed from an isolated, local tool into a worldwide communication station.
- **The large-scale adoption of new technologies:** New information and communication technologies (ICT) like laptops, smartphone and such devices are affordable and reliable. Educational institutions have adopted new

technologies as follows from the widespread connections to the internet, the increased number of school websites and e-learning tools for content management.

Computers/laptops and mobile phones became personal devices. They provide ubiquitous access; they became portable or even wearable or they are seamlessly integrated with environment. Their use gets fully integrated in our daily activities and they literally become extensions of our physical and mental being. Technology Enhanced Learning (TEL) is important for many reasons. It is not only important because it is the standard of education that is expected today, but it can also improve education. The word COME can reveal the why aspect more clearly; C-Content, O-Objective, M-Medium/ method and E-Evaluation.

**Content:** Content of curriculum is always the important factor in education. Technology enhanced learning strengthens this. The following are features of TEL

- Authorities are there to provide content, but learners, both students and teachers can make use of additional reference.
- More resources
- Watch again
- Knowledge is open for all, for students and even for public
- Knowledge in fingertips
- Research and innovation

**Objectives:** There are different objectives for learning, set by authorities which includes learn technology during and after learning, which is necessary to succeed in the world. The objectives include,

- Learns at students' own pace
- Keeps engaged
- Irrespective of space
- Mass education, in-formal, nonformal etc

**Medium/Methods:** Technology also functions as a medium or method. Online classes and recorded (Synchronised and asynchronised) classes are very popular in these days. The transition of medium is from print to electronic, the contribution of Guttenberg and

- Activity theory

- Technology functions as a method for both teaching and learning.
- Synchronised and asynchronised (live and recorded)

**Evaluation:** Evaluation can be done with the help of technology, both offline and online mode. Now it is common in school education, higher education and other various types of competitive examination.

- Provision for self-assessment both for students and teachers. E.g. recorded classes, evaluation tools/feedback forms etc
- The concept of paper less examination
- Can save time, energy etc
- easy for answer script valuation
- easy for publishing results
- certificates also can be printed easily

## CLOUD COMPUTING

The term Cloud refers to a Network or Internet. Cloud can provide services over network, i.e., on public networks or on private networks, i.e., WAN, LAN or VPN Applications such as e-mail, web conferencing, customer relationship management (CRM), all run in cloud. Cloud Computing refers to manipulating, configuring, and accessing the applications online. It offers online data storage, infrastructure and application. We need not to install a piece of software on our local PC and this is how the cloud computing overcomes platform dependency issues. Hence, the Cloud Computing is making our business application mobile and collaborative.

### Characteristics of Cloud Computing

- **On Demand Self-Service:** Cloud Computing allows the users to use web services and resources on demand. One can logon to a website at any time and use them
- **Broad Network Access:** Since Cloud Computing is completely web based, it can be accessed from anywhere and at any time
- **Resource Pooling:** Cloud Computing allows multiple tenants to share a pool of resources. One can share single physical

instance of hardware, database and basic infrastructure

- **Rapid Elasticity:** It is very easy to scale up or down the resources at any time. Resources used by the customers or currently assigned to customers are automatically monitored

**History of Cloud Computing:** The concept of Cloud Computing came into existence in 1950 with implementation of mainframe computers, accessible via thin/static clients. Since then, cloud computing has been evolved from static clients to dynamic ones from software to services.

## Benefits of Cloud Computing

- One can access applications as utilities, over the Internet
- Manipulate and configure the application online at any time
- It does not require to install a specific piece of software to access or manipulate cloud application
- Cloud Computing offers online development and deployment tools, programming runtime environment through
- Platform as a Service model
- Cloud resources are available over the network in a manner that provides platform independent access to any type of clients
- Cloud Computing offers on-demand self-service. The resources can be used without interaction with cloud service provider
- Cloud Computing is highly cost effective because it operates at higher efficiencies with greater utilization. It just requires an Internet connection
- Cloud Computing offers load balancing that makes it more reliable.

## Risks of Cloud Computing

Although Cloud Computing is a great innovation in the world of computing, there also exist downsides of cloud computing, viz.

- **Security and Privacy**: It is the biggest concern about cloud computing. Since data management and infrastructure management in cloud is provided by third-party, it is always a risk to handover the sensitive information to such providers. Although the cloud computing vendors ensure more secure password protected accounts, any sign of security breach would result in loss of clients and businesses.

- **Lock-In**: It is very difficult for the customers to switch from one Cloud Service Provider (CSP) to another. It results in dependency on a particular CSP for service.
- **Isolation Failure:** This risk involves the failure of isolation mechanism that separates storage, memory, routing between the different tenants.
- **Management Interface Compromise:** In case of public cloud provider, the customer management interfaces are accessible through the Internet.
- **Insecure or Incomplete Data Deletion:** It is possible that the data requested for deletion may not get deleted. It happens either because extra copies of data are stored but are not available or disk destroyed also stores data from other tenants.

## Basic Concepts of Cloud Computing

There are certain services and models working behind the scene making the cloud computing feasible and accessible to end users. Following are the working models for cloud computing: Deployment Models and Service Models. Deployment models define the type of access to the cloud, i.e., how the cloud is located? Cloud can have any of the four types of access: Public, Private, Hybrid and Community.

## PUBLIC CLOUD

The Public Cloud allows systems and services to be easily accessible to the general public. Public cloud may be less secure because of its openness. E.g. Google, Amazon, Microsoft offers cloud services via Internet. The benefits of public cloud model are:

- **Cost Effective**: Since public cloud share same resources with large number of consumers, it has low cost.
- **Reliability:** Public cloud employs large number of resources from different locations, if any of the resource fail, public cloud can employ another one.
- **Flexibility**: It is also very easy to integrate public cloud with

private cloud, hence gives consumers a flexible approach.

- **Location Independence**: public cloud services are delivered through Internet, therefore ensures location independence
- **Utility Style Costing**: It is based on pay-per-use model and resources are accessible whenever consumer needs it
- **High Scalability**: Cloud resources are made available on demand from a pool of resources, i.e., they can be scaled up or down according the requirement.

**Disadvantages:**

- **Low Security**: In public cloud model, data is hosted off-site and resources are shared publicly, therefore does not ensure higher level of security.
- **Less Customizable**: It is comparatively less customizable than private cloud.

## PRIVATE CLOUD

It allows systems and services to be accessible within an organization. It offers increased security because of its private nature. The Private Cloud is operated only within a single organization. It may be managed internally or by third-party. There are many benefits of deploying cloud as private cloud model, viz.

- **Higher Security and Privacy:** Private cloud operations are not available to general public and resources are shared from distinct pool of resources, therefore, ensures high security and privacy.
- **More Control:** Private clouds have more control on its resources and hardware than public cloud because it is accessed only within an organization
- **Cost And Energy Efficiency:** Private cloud resources are not as cost effective as public clouds but they offer more efficiency than public cloud Disadvantages
- **Restricted Area**: Private cloud is only accessible locally and is very difficult to deploy globally.
- **Inflexible Pricing:** In order to fulfil demand, purchasing new hardware is very costly.

- **Limited Scalability**: Private cloud can be scaled only within capacity of internal hosted resources.
- **Additional Skills:** In order to maintain cloud deployment, organization requires more skilled and expertise.

## COMMUNITY CLOUD

The Community Cloud allows systems and services to be accessible by group of organization. It shares the infrastructure between several organizations from a specific community. It may be managed internally or by the third-party.

### Benefits of Community Cloud

- Cost Effective: Sharing Between Organizations Community cloud provides an infrastructure to share cloud resources and capabilities among several organizations
- Security: Community cloud is comparatively more secure than the public cloud

### Issues of Community Cloud

- Since all data is housed at one location, one must be careful in storing data in community cloud because it might be accessible by others
- It is also challenging to allocate responsibilities of governance, security and cost.

## HYBRID CLOUD

The Hybrid Cloud is mixture of public and private cloud. The critical activities are performed using private cloud while the non-critical activities are performed using public cloud

### Benefits of Hybrid Cloud

- **Scalability:** It offers both features of public cloud scalability and private cloud scalability
- **Flexibility:** It offers both secure resources and scalable public resources.
- **Cost Efficiencies**: Public cloud is more cost effective than private, therefore hybrid cloud can have this saving

- **Security:** Private cloud in hybrid cloud ensures higher degree of security

### Disadvantages of Hybrid Cloud

- **Networking Issues:** Networking becomes complex due to presence of private and public cloud.
- **Security Compliance:** It is necessary to ensure that cloud services are compliant with organization's security policies.
- **Infrastructural Dependency:** The hybrid cloud model is dependent on internal IT infrastructure; therefore, it is necessary to ensure redundancy across data centres.

## SERVICE MODELS

Service Models are the reference models on which the Cloud Computing is based. These can be categorized into three basic service models, such as (a) Infrastructure as a Service (IaaS), (b) Platform as a Service (PaaS), and (c) Software as a Service (SaaS).

**Infrastructure as a Service (IaaS):** It accesses to fundamental resources such as physical machines, virtual machines, virtual storage, etc. Apart from these resources, the IaaS also offers:

- Virtual machine disk storage
- Virtual local area network (VLANs)
- Load balancers
- IP addresses
- Software bundles

All of the above resources are made available to end user via server virtualization. Moreover, these resources are accessed the customers as if they own them.

### Characteristics of IaaS service model:

- Virtual machines with pre-installed software.
- Virtual machines with pre-installed Operating Systems such as Windows, Linux, and Solaris.
- On-demand availability of resources.
- Allows to store copies of particular data in different locations.

- The computing resources can be easily scaled up and down Benefits IaaS:
- It allows the cloud provider to freely locate the infrastructure over the Internet in a cost-effective manner.
- Full Control of the computing resources through Administrative Access to VMs.
- Flexible and Efficient renting of Computer Hardware.
- Portability, Inter-operability with Legacy Applications.

**Platform as a Service (PaaS):** PaaS offers the runtime environment for applications. It also offers development and deployment tools, required to develop applications. PaaS has a feature of point-and-click tools that enables non-developers to create web applications. E.g. Google's App Engine, Force.com. Developer may log on to these websites and use the built-in API to create web-based applications. But the disadvantage of using PaaS is that the developer lock-in with a particular vendor. For example, an application written in Python against Google's API using Google's App Engine is likely to work only in that environment. Therefore, the vendor lock-in is the biggest problem in PaaS.

## Benefits of PaaS

- **Lower Administrative Overhead**: Consumer need not to bother much about the administration because it's the responsibility of cloud provider.
- **Lower Total Cost of Ownership**: Consumer need not purchase expensive hardware, servers.
- **More Current System Software**: It is the responsibility of the cloud provider to maintain software versions and patch installations. Issues Like SaaS, PaaS also place significant burdens on consumer's browsers to maintain reliable and secure connections to the provider systems ISSUES
- **Lack of Portability Between PaaS Clouds**: Although standard languages are used yet the implementations of platforms services may vary. For example, file, queue, or hash table interfaces of one platform may differ from another, making it difficult to transfer workloads from one platform to another.

- **Event Based Processor Scheduling**: The PaaS applications are event oriented which poses resource constraints on applications, i.e., they have to answer a request in a given interval of time.
- **Security Engineering of PaaS Applications**: Since the PaaS applications are dependent on network, PaaS applications must explicitly use cryptography and manage security exposures.

## Software as a Service (SaaS)

This model allows to provide software application as a service to the end users. It refers to a software that is deployed on a hosted service and is accessible via Internet. There are several SaaS applications, some of them are listed below:

- Billing and Invoicing System
- Customer Relationship Management (CRM) applications
- Help Desk Applications
- Human Resource (HR)

## Characteristics of SaaS

- SaaS makes the software available over the Internet.
- The Software are maintained by the vendor rather than where they are running
- The license to the software may be subscription based or usage based. And it is billed on recurring basis.
- SaaS applications are cost effective since they do not require any maintenance at end user side.
- They are available on demand.
- They can be scaled up or down on demand.
- They are automatically upgraded and updated.
- SaaS offers share data model. Therefore, multiple users can share single instance of infrastructure. It is not required to hard code the functionality for individual users.
- All users are running same version of the software.

## Benefits of Using SaaS

- **Modest Software Tools:** The SaaS application deployment requires a little or no client-side software installation which results in the following benefits: No requirement for complex software packages at client side Little or no risk of configuration at client-side Low distribution cost
- **Efficient use of Software Licenses:** The client can have single license for multiple computers running at different locations which reduces the licensing cost. Also, there is no requirement for license servers because the software runs in the provider's infrastructure.
- **Centralized Management and Data:** The data stored by the cloud provider is centralised. However, the cloud providers may store data in a decentralised manner for sake of redundancy and reliability.
- **Platform Responsibilities managed by Providers:** All platform responsibilities such as backups, system maintenance, security, hardware refresh, power management, etc., are performed by the cloud provider. The consumer need not to bother about them.
- **Multitenant Solutions:** Multitenancy allows multiple users to share single instance of resources in virtual isolation.
- Consumers can customize their application without affecting the core functionality
- There are many other service models all of which can take the form like XaaS, i.e., Anything as a Service.
- This can be Network as a Service, Business as a Service, Identity as a Service, Database as a Service or Strategy as a Service

## CLOUD COMPUTING-TECHNOLOGIES

There are certain technologies that are working behind the cloud computing platforms making cloud computing flexible, reliable, usable. These technologies are; Virtualization, Service-Oriented Architecture (SOA), Grid Computing, Utility Computing, and Virtualization. Virtualization is a technique, which allows to share single physical instance of an application or resource among multiple organizations or tenants (customers). It does so by assigning a logical name to a physical resource and providing a pointer to that physical resource when demanded. The Multitenant architecture offers virtual isolation among the multiple tenants and therefore the organizations can use and customize the application as though they each have its own instance running

**Service-Oriented Architecture (SOA)** helps to use applications as a service for other applications regardless the type of vendor, product or technology. It is possible to exchange of data between applications of different vendors without additional programming or making changes to services.

**Grid Computing** refers to distributed computing in which a group of computers from multiple locations are connected with each other to achieve common objective. These computer resources are heterogeneous and geographically dispersed. Grid Computing breaks complex task into smaller pieces. These smaller pieces are distributed to CPUs that reside within the grid.

**Utility Computing** is based on Pay per Use model. It offers computational resources on demand as a metered service. Cloud computing, grid computing, and managed IT services are based on the concept of Utility computing

**Cloud Computing Architecture:** It comprises of many cloud components, each of them is loosely coupled. We can broadly divide the cloud architecture into two parts: Front End and Back End. Each of the ends are connected through a network, usually via Internet. Front End refers to the client part of cloud computing system. e.g., Web Browser. Back End refers to the cloud itself.

- **Identity-as-a-Service**: Employees in a company require to login into system to perform various tasks. These systems may be based on local server or cloud based. IDaaS offers management of identity (information) as a digital entity. This identity can be used during electronic transactions. Identity refers to set of attributes associated with something and make it recognizable. All objects may have same attributes, but their identity cannot be the same. This unique identity is assigned through unique identification attribute.

- **Single Sign-On (SSO):** To solve the problem of using different username & password combination for different servers, companies now employ Single Sign-On software, which allows the user to login only one time and manages the user's access to other systems. SSO has single authentication server, managing multiple accesses to other systems
- **Cloud Computing Data Storage:** Cloud Storage is a service that allows to save data on offsite storage system managed by third-party and is made accessible by a web services API.
- **Storage Devices:** Storage devices can be broadly classified into two categories: Block Storage Devices File Storage Devices. **Block Storage Devices** offer raw storage to the clients. This raw storage can be partitioned to create volumes. **File Storage Devices** offers storage to clients in form of files, maintaining its own file system. This storage is in the form of Network Attached Storage (NAS).
- **Cloud Computing Security:** Security in cloud computing is a major concern. Data in cloud should be stored in encrypted form. To restrict client from direct accessing the shared data, proxy and brokerage services should be employed.
- **Security Planning:** Before deploying a particular resource to cloud, one should need to analyse several attributes about the resource such as: Select which resources he is going to move to cloud and analyse its sensitivity to risk. Consider cloud service models require consumer to be responsible for security at different levels of service. Consider which cloud type such as public, private, community or hybrid. Understand the cloud service provider's system that how data is transferred, where it is stored and how to move data into and out of cloud.

## Cloud Computing Operations

Cloud Computing operation refers to delivering superior cloud service. These operations can be performed using a web application or mobile based applications. There are a number of operations that are performed in cloud content management, e-mail marketing, accounting services, online market place, human resource management etc.

## Cloud Computing Applications

Cloud Computing has its applications in almost all the fields such as business, entertainment, data storage, social networking, management, entertainment, education, art and global positioning system, etc. Some of the widely famous cloud computing applications are discussed here:

- **MailChimp,** it offers an e-mail publishing platform. It is widely employed by the businesses to design and send their e-mail campaigns.
- **Chatter** app helps the employee to share important information about organization in real time. One can get the instant feed regarding any issue.
- **Google Apps for Business** Google offers creating text documents, spreadsheets, presentations, etc., on Google Docs which allows the business users to share them in collaborating manner.
- **QuickBooks** It offers online accounting solutions for a business. It helps in monitoring cash flow, creating VAT returns and creating business reports.

## Data Storage and Backup

- **Box.com** offers drag and drop service for files. It just required to drop the files into Box and access from anywhere.
- **Mozy** offers online backup service for files during a data loss.
- **Joukuu** is a web-based interface. It allows to display a single list of contents for files stored in Google Docs, Box.net and Dropbox.

**Management Applications:** There are apps available for management task such as time tracking, organizing notes.

- **Toggl** helps in tracking time period assigned to a particular project.
- **Evernote** is an application that organizes the sticky notes and even can read the text from images which helps the user to locate the notes easily.
- **Outright** It is an accounting app. It helps to track income, expenses, profits and losses in real time.

## Social Applications

- Facebook offers social networking service. One can share photos, videos, files, status and much more.
- Twitter helps to interact directly with the public. One can follow any celebrity, organization and any person, who is on twitter and can have latest updates regarding the same. Entertainment Applications
- Audiobox.fm offers streaming service, i.e., music can be stored online and can be played from cloud using service's own media player.
- Art Applications like Moo offers art services such as designing and printing business cards, and postcards

## Cloud Computing Providers

- **Salesforce.com** This is a Force.com development platform. This provides a simple user interface and lets users log in, build an app and push it in the cloud.
- The **Appistry'sCloudQ** platform is efficient in delivering a runtime application platform. This platform is very useful to create scalable and service-oriented applications.
- The **AppScale** is an open-source platform for Google App Engine applications.
- The **AT&T** allows access to virtual servers and manages the virtualization infrastructure. This virtualization infrastructure includes network, server and storage.
- The **Engine Yard** is a Rails Application cloud computing platform.
- The **Enomaly** provides the infrastructure-as-a-Service platform.
- The **FlexiScale** offers a cloud computing platform that allows flexible, scalable and automated cloud infrastructure.
- The **GCloud3** offers private cloud solution in its g Platform.
- The **Gizmox** Visual WebGUI platform is best suited for developing new web apps and modernize the legacy apps based on ASP.net, DHTML, etc.

- The **GoGrid** platform allows the users to deploy web and database cloud services.

## Cloud Computing Providers

- The **Google**'s App Engine lets the users build, run and maintain their applications on Google's infrastructure.
- The **LongJump** offers a Business Application Platform, a platform-as-a-Service (PaaS).
- The Microsoft's **Windows Azure** is a cloud computing platform offering an environment to create cloud apps and services.
- **OrangeScape** offers a Platform-as-a-Service (PaaS) for non-programmers. Building an app is as easy as spreadsheet.
- The **RackSpace** provide servers-on-demand via a cloud-driven platform of virtualized servers.
- The **Amazon EC2** (Elastic Compute Cloud) lets the users configure and control computing resources while running them on Amazon's environment.

**Cloud Computing Challenges:** Cloud Computing, an emergence technology, has placed many challenges in different aspects:

- **Security and Privacy** of information is the biggest challenge to cloud computing. Security and privacy issues can be overcome by employing encryption, security hardware and security applications.
- **Portability**: This is another challenge to cloud computing that applications should easily be migrated from one cloud provider to another. There should not be vendor lock-in. However, it is not yet made possible because each of the cloud provider uses different standard languages for their platforms.

# MOBILE CLOUD COMPUTING

Cloud Computing offers such smartphones that have rich Internet media experience and require less processing, less power. In term of Mobile Cloud Computing, processing is done in cloud, data is stored in cloud. And the mobile devices serve as a media for display. Today smartphones are employed with rich cloud services by integrating applications that consume web services. These web services are deployed in cloud. There are several Smartphone operating systems available such as Google's Android, Apple's iOS, RIM BlackBerry, Symbian, and Windows Mobile Phone. Each of these platforms support third-party applications that are deployed in cloud.

## M-LEARNING

The evolution of handheld portable devices and wireless technology has resulted in radical changes in the social and economic lifestyles of modern people. Today, many technological devices are produced in portable form and people have become accustomed to them. These devices are reshaping users' daily lives in different ways. But the development of digital technologies has so far been limited to social communication and few people have regarded mobile learning as a core pedagogical activity in higher institutions of learning. Although this model has been used as a minor adjunct to learning activities such as lectures and assignments, it is still not the primary mode of delivery in higher education. Currently, the instructional technology transmitted by means of mobile technology is mainly social and, to a lesser extent, economic. Advanced mobile devices such as "smart" cellular telephones are very popular among people primarily because they are wireless and portable. These functionalities enable users to communicate while on the move. The popularity of these devices is therefore a consequent of their ability to function at multiple levels. Moreover, the intense commercial competitiveness in the mobile device industry is forcing manufacturers to be very innovative, constantly striving to introduce new features that can give them a competitive edge. Against this backdrop, visionary educators, designers and developers should begin to consider the implications of these devices for the modern teaching and learning environment. In such an environment, contents and services can be relayed to a university student by personal wireless mobile devices. This will add another layer to the personal computer-based model of teaching and learning. This also means e-learning will take place in conditions that will be radically different from those educators and learners are familiar with. Providing university students with services, content instruction and information outside the traditional learning space is becoming more acceptable among education providers who predicate their services on the routine use of advanced information and communication technologies. The emergence of revolutionary technologies has had a significant impact on educational technology. It has increased the potential of e-learning as a mode of delivery in education.

## Concept of M-learning

In general, mobile learning (or m-learning) can be viewed as any form of learning that happens when mediated through a mobile device, and a form of learning that established the legitimacy of 'nomadic' learners (Alexander, 2004). The kind of informal learning through the use of mobile devices makes it an even more potent tool of educational communication than the customary forms and modes of traditional education.

## Definitions of M-learning

Any type of learning that takes place in learning environments and spaces that take account of the mobility of technology, mobility of learners and mobility of learning" (Baran, 2014, p.20). "Mobile learning (or m-learning) is learning by means of wireless technological devices that can be pocketed and utilised wherever the learner's device is able to receive unbroken transmission signals" (Attewell & Savill-Smith, 2005). Traxler (2007) define mobile learning as "wireless and digital devices and technologies, generally produced for the public, used by a learner as he or she participates in higher education. Others define and conceptualise mobile learning by placing a strong emphasis on the mobility of learners and the mobility of learning, and the experiences of learners as they learn by means of mobile devices".

## Theoretical Overview of M-learning

According to Naismith et al. (2004) use of mobile technology in education can be categorised into six main themes:

1. **Behaviourist** — activities that promote learning as a change in observable actions (drill and feedback model).
2. **Constructivist** — activities in which learners actively construct new ideas or concepts based on both their previous and current knowledge (participatory and interactive model).
3. **Situated** — activities that promote learning within an

authentic context and culture (authentic and contextual model).

4. **Collaborative** — activities that promote learning through social interaction (conversational and shared model).
5. **Informal and lifelong** — activities that support learning outside a dedicated learning environment and formal curriculum (personalised, outside formal application model).
6. **Learning and teaching support** — activities that assist in the co-ordination of learners and resources for learning activities (learning support model for academic, administrative and technical purposes).

**Features of M-learning:** According to (Huang, Huang & Hsieh, 2008, p, 3) the features of M-learning include:

- enhancing availability and accessibility of information networks
- engaging students in learning-related activities in diverse physical locations
- supporting of project-based group work
- improving of communication and collaborative learning in the classroom, and
- enabling quick content delivery

However, mobile learning provides the support for learning and training, and "mobile technologies have contributed to the potential to support learners studying a variety of subjects" (Järvelä, Näykki, Laru, & Luokkanen, 2007, p. 71).

## Different types of M-learning

From a developing country perspective, features such as limited or no dependence on permanent electricity supply, easy maintenance, easy-to-use audio and text interfaces, affordability and accessibility are the most important considerations for using mobile phones as potential learning tools. Based on the use pattern, Traxler (2007) has categorised mobile learning as:

- **Technology-driven mobile learning** — Some specific technological innovation is deployed in an academic setting to demonstrate technical feasibility and pedagogic possibility.

- **Miniature but portable e-learning** — Mobile, wireless and hand-held technologies are used to re-enact approaches and solutions already used in "conventional" e-learning, to provide access to some virtual learning environment (VLE) using mobile technologies as flexible replacements for desktop technologies.
- **Connected classroom learning** — The same technologies are used in classroom settings to support collaborative learning, perhaps connected to other classroom technologies such as interactive whiteboards.
- **Informal, personalised, situated mobile learning** — The same technologies are enhanced with additional functionality (for example, location-awareness or video-capture) and deployed to deliver educational experiences that would otherwise be difficult or impossible.
- **Mobile training or performance support** — The technologies are used to improve the productivity and efficiency of mobile workers by delivering information and support just-in-time and in context for their immediate priorities.
- **Remote, rural or development mobile learning** — The technologies are used to address environmental and infrastructural challenges to deliver and support education where "conventional" e-learning technologies would fail, often troubling accepted developmental or evolutionary paradigms.

**Framework for M-learning:** Koole (2009) has proposed a framework for understanding mobile learning. According to this framework, mobile learning falls within the intersection of learner, device and social aspects as represented in Figure 10.1. The labels in the illustration can be explained as follows:

- **Device Aspect** — refers to size, weight, input or output capabilities, file storage and retrieval, processor speed of the equipment.
- **Learner Aspect** — refers to their prior knowledge, memory, context and transfer, discovery learning, emotions and motivations.

- **Social Aspect** — refers to conversations, co-operation and social interactions among users.
- **Social Technology (DS) intersection** — refers to device networking, system connectivity and collaboration tools.
- **Interaction Learning (LS) intersection** — refers to interaction, situated cognition and learning communities.
- **Device Usability (DL) intersection** — refers to portability, information availability, psychological comfort and satisfaction.
- **Mobile Learning (DLS)** — refers to information access and selection, mediation and knowledge navigation in mobile learning

## Different Concepts of M-learning

The portability and mobility of these technological devices have had strong implications for the meaning of terms that had been extensively defined in existing literature. Using the mobile device as a signifier, the concepts of mobility can be divided into three significant areas: mobility of technology, mobility of learner and mobility of learning especially in higher education landscape. This tripartite division of mobility is evident in the current literature on the subject and designers who have used mobile technology for educational purposes have confirmed this. Figure 1 is a graphic depiction of the three divisions of mobile devices that can deliver a higher level of educational instruction. In practice, the technology, the learner and the actual learning process operate in an uninterrupted continuum within the social context of education. The successful delivery of higher educational instruction depends on the tripartite significance of the word mobility as it is used in the context of higher education. These three elements are interdependent and are equally important in making mobile devices viable as instruments for the delivery of higher education instructional contents. Accordingly, Baran (2014) define "mobile learning as learning environmental based on mobility of technology, mobility of learners and mobility of learning that augments the higher educational landscape".

## Mobility of Technology

The mobile technology is mainly more advanced cellular

telephones. But there are other forms of technology such as "smart" phones, digital cameras, flash-discs, iPods and personal digital assistance devices (PDAs). Mobile devices used to deliver higher education content and instruction can also function as audio-players, media-players and digital cameras. Advanced mobile devices are furnished with Wireless Application Protocol (WAP) and Wireless Fidelity (Wi-Fi) capacities so that a user can connect to the Internet by means of his or her PDA (Trinder, 2005). The mobile cellular devices mentioned above have the capacity to link to the Internet and deliver content and instruction that can enable learners to learn at anytime and anywhere in a format that is culturally prestigious among people in the same age group.

Most of the more advanced models can support a portable, digital and wireless lifestyle and mode of teaching and learning. It is precisely the mobility of these devices that makes them highly prestigious and therefore desirable as instruments of learning among learners in the same age group. In fact, they are highly valued by young people in their early twenties because they are visible indicators of wealth, privilege, luxury and modernity. Mobile devices with advanced features like those mentioned above are therefore regarded as more trendy, fashionable and prestigious among these consumers than the standard desktop personal computers that connect to the Internet by means of landlines. The first designers of this mode of delivery were extremely ingenious in the way in which they exploited the prestige and iconic value of mobile devices among young people in their twenties. Educationists have in effect adroitly utilised one of the most potent symbols of wealth, prestige and fashion among the young. Education by means of mobile devices is therefore nothing if not revolutionary in its design methods, implications and results.

Trinder (2005, pp. 7-8) explains the functionalities of the most popular and expensive mobile phone technologies. These include an organiser, video camera, telephone, GPS and film player. They also include games, e-book, e-mail facility Internet access and musical MP3s. But the most popular functions in all mobile phone remain the short messaging service (SMS) and the multimedia messaging service (MMS) – frequently used functions in the delivery of higher education instructions. This innovation has been discussed in terms of Trinder's (2005) classification of PDA functionality.

The Personal Digital Assistant (PDA) device connects easily with the Internet, and enabling it to perform many different functions. (Kukulska-Hulme & Traxler, 2005, p. 2): Also "when combined with wireless connectivity, learning activities can be monitored and coordinated between locations. However, the task of designing such activities and appropriate learner support is complex and challenging. The impacts of new mobile technologies need to be appraised and evaluated" (Kukulska-Hulme & Traxler, 2005, p. 2). This is because of the challenges that still have to be overcome before this mode of educational delivery becomes as widely accepted as e-learning. However, Motiwalla (2007) states that although it is inevitable that m-learning will soon become an essential extension of e-learning, this transition will not happen overnight. Instant access to learning at any time and in many places will obviously be very useful to learners, but only to a privileged few until wireless technology becomes more efficient and widely available. It also depends on designers' ability to apply the appropriate forms of instruction that will make this mode of learning an essential tool in the delivery of higher education. From a technological point of view, mobile devices are becoming more and more capable of performing all the functions necessary in learning design. Since affordability and sophistication of mobile device technology have increased its popularity within the educational context and, educationalists should determine whether current theories of psychological, educational learning and instructional design are adequate to describe the processes and meet the challenges posed by this new mode of delivery. Traxler (2007) writes: "[designers have] not explored the actual technologies or pedagogies in any detail and [have] sought to define questions for discussion rather than provide answers for what might in fact be premature or inappropriate questions".

## Mobility of Learners

E-learning mediated by personal computers is mostly bound by location and time (availability) because of the configuration of a personal computer. The computer has no wireless learning tool linked to the Internet, which means that one must always work in one place at a particular time determined by availability and connectivity. But with mobile learning, learning can occur at any place and at any time. The ordinary (non-mobile) personal computer with landline connections to the Internet is constrained by the places in which they are located and their availability. Nonportable personal computers are too heavy to move easily and so learners are compelled to work in the same place and during the time slots allocated to them by university authorities. By contrast, learning with mobile is a learner centric activity because it is both mobile and nomadic, and not pedagogically teacher-centric as in the case of traditional lectures and hardware installed in one particular location under the aegis of the university's authorities.

Ting (2005) makes the following remarks about the advantages of mobile learning: "The overall advantages provided by the mobile learning are [that it is characterised by] more flexible, accessible and personalised learning activities. Such advantages […] keep the learners engaged in the ongoing learning activities and enhance their productivity and effectiveness". Furthermore, Guralnich (2008) suggests that the designer would be better served if he/she considered the entire context in which learners will use particular m-learning programme. However, today's designers often tend to borrow design ideas from their e-learning experience.

Mobile learning devices also have the capacity to enhance a learner's sense of individuality and community as well as his or her motivation to learn through participation in collaborative learning. These devices stimulate a learner's sense of ownership of the content as he/she participates actively in a variety of social, collaborative and cooperative activities - all of which are centred on the mobile learning device. Educators and designers should address the needs of learners in this age of wireless communication and connectedness. Slogans such as "walk and use", "walk and talk", "just for me" and "just in time" usher in the new phrases in education like "You ring, we bring" ushered in previous developments in society. Instructional theory in this mobile age should be learner-centric rather than technology- or teacher-centric. This is because, as Uden (2007) observes: "Mobile technologies offer new opportunities for students' educational activities in that they can be used across different locations and times". Students using mobile technologies are not only remote from their instructors; they also fully control the access of information on their mobile devices. In this light, one of the main advantages of mobile learning is that it allows this generation of learners to enjoy a certain amount of freedom and independence.

## Mobility of Learning

Researchers and practitioners of mobile learning are engaged in pioneering experiments for transmitting the full content of higher learning to students by means of mobile cellular devices. Walker (2007) points out that the advantages of mobile learning are not dependent solely upon the ability to use a portable and wireless communication device successfully. He argues that the kind of learning experienced by mobile owners is unique because it is received and processed within the context in which the learner is situated. The context is utterly individual – completely different from the rigid outlay of the traditional classroom or lecture room, and the computer laboratory.

The international conference on mobile learning entitled MLearn 2004 adopted as its guiding statement the desire to provide "learning anytime and everywhere", Attewell & Savill-Smith (2005)'s paper and those of other contributions were designed to indicate how such a vision could be fulfilled. Most of the papers presented at this conference focused on the description and development of theories that would support the practice of mobile learning and the design production of mobile learning materials and systems.

Mobile learning devices have also enriched the theory and practice of e-learning. Contemporary consumers of higher education in developing countries almost always use mobile learning devices as adjuncts to e-learning in higher education. Sophisticated mobile devices are currently capable of delivering a comprehensive range of e-learning materials by means of web connections, infrared and Bluetooth transmissions. For Ally (2005) "mobile learning [is at the] intersection of mobile computing and e-learning; [it provides] accessible resources wherever you are, strong search capabilities, rich interaction, powerful support for effective learning and performance-based assessment".

## Learning cycle of M-learning

Shih (2005) presents a modified ARCS model for designing m-learning that can be considered an instructional design approach. The learning cycle in the Shih's model as shown in Figure shown below includes:

- sending a multimedia message to mobile phones to trigger

and motivate learners;

- searching the Web for related information by using hyperlinks (URLs) embedded in the message received;
- discussing with learning peers by text, voice, picture or video messaging;
- producing a digital story that tells what they learn through an audio or video diary (a moblogging journal); and
- applying what they learn in a simulated environment such as online educational gaming.

## Reasons for use of M-learning in different contexts

Kukulska-Hulme and Traxler (2005) reveal the reasons of m-learning use in several different contexts. Regarding, **Access** m-learning improving access to assessment, learning materials and learning resources; m-learning increasing flexibility of learning for students; and m-learning compliance with special educational needs and disability legislation.

## Changes in teaching and learning

- exploring the potential for collaborative learning, for increasing students' appreciation of their own learning process and for consolidation of learning;
- guiding students to see a subject differently than they would have done without the use of mobile devices;
- identifying learners' needs for just-in-time knowledge;
- exploring whether the time and task management facilities of mobile devices can help students to manage their studies;
- reducing cultural and communication barriers between staff and students by using channels that students like; and
- wanting to know how wireless or mobile technology alters attitudes, patterns of study and communication activity among students.

## Alignment with institutional or business aims

- making wireless, mobile, interactive learning available to all students without incurring the expense of costly hardware;

- delivering communications, information and training to large numbers of people regardless of their location;
- blending mobile technologies into e-learning infrastructures to improve interactivity and connectivity for the learner; and
- harnessing the existing proliferation of mobile phone services and their many users.

## M-Learning in Teacher Education

The purpose of higher education and the relatively new ubiquity of mobile devices in our culture have imbued the mobile device with new meanings. Higher education can now be presented in a more sustained and interactive fashion to empower those who need it. Mobile devices have become attractive learning devices for education. While the majority of the existing research has focused primarily on the value of mobile learning for students, researchers have recently started exploring its potentials within teacher development. The present qualitative synthesis of quantitative and qualitative research aimed to address trends and gaps observed in the literature regarding the integration of mobile learning into teacher education. Six main findings emerged: (a) there is an increasing trend in integrating mobile learning in teacher education contexts; (b) theoretical and conceptual perspectives are scarcely reported; (c) variations exist in perceptions, attitudes and usage patterns; (d) engagement with mobile learning and devices is primarily reported as being beneficial; (e) challenges were scarcely reported; and (f) several pedagogical affordances support mobile learning integration into teacher education settings. These findings have been interpreted to determine their implications on the development of mobile learning experiences in teacher education, including programmatic directions for integration and study.

## Approaches in M-learning

**Classroom:** Applications in classrooms and other learning spaces combine the use of handheld computers, PDAs, smartphones or handheld voting systems (such as clickers) with traditional resources (Tremblay 2010).

**Class management:** Mobile devices in brick-and-mortar classrooms can be used to enhance student-centred learning, group collaboration among students through communication applications, interactive displays, Quick response codes and video features.

- Existing mobile technology can replace cumbersome resources such as textbooks, visual aids, and presentation technology.
- Interactive and multi-mode technology allows students to engage and manipulate information.
- Mobile Device features with WIFI capabilities allow for on-demand access to information.
- Access to classroom activities and information on mobile devices provides a continuum for learning inside and outside the classroom.

In a literature review conducted by *FutureLab*, researchers found that increased communication, collaboration, and understanding of concepts was a result of mobile technology applications.

**Distance Learning:** Mobile devices can be used in online settings to enhance learning experiences.

- The mobile phone (through text SMS notices) can be used especially for distance education or with students whose courses require them to be highly mobile and in particular to communicate information regarding availability of assignment results, venue changes and cancellations, etc.
- Mobile devices facilitate online interaction between teacher and student, and student to student. Mobile devices make it possible to facilitate interaction in real time, allowing students to obtain immediate feedback. Educators can also assess student comprehension by using mobile devices, which provide real time updates on student progress, enabling teachers to adapt and personalize their teaching.
- It can also be of value to business people, e.g. sales representatives who do not wish to waste time away from their busy schedules to attend formal training events.

**Podcasting:** Podcasting consists of listening to audio recordings of lectures. It can be used to review live lectures (Clark & Westcott 2007) and to provide opportunities for students to rehearse oral presentations. Podcasts may also provide supplemental information to enhance traditional lectures (McGarr 2009) (Steven & Teasley 2009).

## Strengths and Limitations

Some key advantages of mobile learning include the following (Attewell, 2005):

- allows truly anywhere, anytime, personalised learning;
- can be used to enliven, or add variety to, conventional lessons or courses;
- can be used to remove some of the formality which non-traditional learners may find unattractive or frightening and can make learning fun;
- can help deliver and support literacy, numeracy and language learning;
- can help learners and teachers to recognise and build on existing basic literacy skills which allow young people to communicate in notational form via text messages;
- facilitates both individual and collaborative learning experiences; M-Learning
- enables discrete learning in the sensitive area of literacy;
- can help to combat resistance to the use of ICT by providing a bridge between mobile phone literacy and PC literacy;
- has been observed to help young disconnected learners to remain more focused for longer periods; and
- can help to raise self-confidence and self-esteem by recognising uncelebrated skills, enabling non-threatening, personalised learning experiences and enabling peer-to-peer learning and support.

## Limitations of mobile learning

Most of the limitations of mobile learning are due to the small screen size of the mobile devices and their limited battery life. A study by Doolittle and Mariano (2008) found that learning while mobile was negatively affected in comparison to learning while stationary. They "found that students who learned about historical inquiry using a portable digital media player (e.g., iPod), while navigating a walking course that required attention to the path taken, performed significantly more poorly on measures of recall and transfer than students who learned while simply sitting at a desk" (p. 524). This is a serious drawback, and exclusive use of mobile device for any teaching and learning is therefore not recommended.

Maniar et al. (2008) reported that regardless of the screen size of a mobile device, students tended to have a positive overall opinion of m-learning, and watching a video significantly increased their knowledge of the subject area. However, compared to students who used devices with 2.28-inch to 3.78- inch screens, students who used a device with a 1.65-inch screen had a significantly lower subjective opinion of the screen quality and learned a significantly lower amount. This finding indicates that if an m-learning environment that relies heavily on video-based material is displayed on a device with a 1.65-inch screen, such as an average mobile telephone, then the effectiveness of the learning experience may be inhibited.

Zawacki-Richter et al. (2007) reported that 62 per cent of respondents agreed that screens are currently too small to present complex learning material, and limited battery life of mobile devices was regarded as a problem for extensive use by 59 per cent of respondents. Despite these limitations, 50 per cent of the respondents believed that screen size is not as important as mobile devices should rather be used for communication and interaction purposes rather than for content distribution. Because of the small screen size in mobile devices, the interface should be built in such a way to convey the message using the smallest amount of text, and proper navigation must be built into the system to allow learners to move between screens and sections of the lesson (Ally, 2004). Despite these small limitations, mobile devices should be seen as an opportunity to deliver just-in-time learning and support to learners in remote areas. As Sharples (2003) suggests, rather than seeing mobiles as disruptive devices, educators should seek to exploit the potential of the technology's children bring with them and find ways to put them into good use for the benefit of learning practice.

## Implications of M-learning in teaching and learning

The cell phone is currently the most common platform for m-learning, lending itself to collaborative and project-based efforts that leverage its potential to support the communication requirements of a team. Where wireless networks are available, or where smartphones with data plans have access to cell networks, mobile lessons and exercises can leverage the ability to gather information from a variety of interdisciplinary sources in a wide array of formats while exploiting the value of location-based learning. In developing countries where mobile devices are available at a fraction of the cost of other computing hardware, m-learning has extended the infrastructure of distance education to outlying areas that have previously been poorly served. Regardless of the hardware employed, as demand requires that more applications be re-authored for mobile formats, institutions may find it necessary to overhaul data sharing and content-delivery techniques to support the mobile platform.

Since mobile learning is spreading rapidly and likely to become one of the most efficient ways of delivering higher education instruction in the future, it has become necessary to examine its implication for the design of teaching and learning. The uses and applications of mobile learning have multiplied in different contexts even though the eventual consequences of the proliferation of this medium are not yet entirely clear, either to designers and practitioners themselves or to researchers. It is necessary for research on the effects and modes of mobile learning to investigate and explore the practice of this particular medium in terms of the instructional design theories of the past, and to adapt such theories so that they can account for the extraordinary number of changes that have taken place not only in education, but in society at large. Designers and practitioners of education are therefore responsible to produce coherent and reliable accounts of the likely consequences of the proliferation of mobile devices in the higher education landscape.

The proper design of the technologies leads to greater effectiveness of mobile learning. Such accounts should consider the multiplicity of meanings that are implied by the mobility of educational delivery and the mobility of learners. It is also necessary to describe in detail the various advantages and disadvantages of mobile instructional devices as tools for the delivery of higher education. Philosophers of education should explain the philosophical and theoretical assumptions of mobile learning in higher education. They should also clarify the design paradigm shifts that this mode of delivering higher education has introduced into the world of practice.

## UBIQUITOUS LEARNING (U-LEARNING)

Ubiquitous learning, also called u-learning, is the interaction between humans and computers in order to learn. It's important to note that the term *computers* here don't only refer to desktop and laptop computers. Instead, computers are considered any digital device. However, just having a computer or digital device doesn't make learning ubiquitous. What separates ubiquitous learning from the broader term *e-learning* is that ubiquitous learning evolves learners being constantly in contact with technology always having the ability to learn. In a sense, ubiquitous learning is "learning on demand." This is similar to mobile learning in that the learner is not hindered by his or her location.

### Characteristics of Ubiquitous Learning

Top researchers in ubiquitous learning describe ubiquitous learning as having six characteristics. These are:

- **Permanency:** Both course material and material produced by students is never deleted on purpose; the only time material is deleted is in unforeseen circumstances. Further, students' performance and course materials are continuously being updated.
- **Accessibility**: Because learning data like coursework, assignments, and lectures are permanent, students should always have access to the material. Because this material is accessible, students can be much more self-directed and more independent that previously.
- **Immediacy:** Students should be able to get information whenever they want. The information students request may be local, stored on their device, or not local, the data is most likely stored on a server somewhere and is accessed by the learner over the internet.
- **Interactivity:** Learners should be able to interact with other people in their "educational network." These people can include the teacher of the course, classmates, or even experts in the field. Interactivity can be synchronous, requiring participants to be present at the same time, such as a video

conversation or instant messaging chat room, or asynchronous, such as an uploaded video to YouTube or a forum.

- **Situating of instructional activities:** The problems and knowledge gained from learning activities are presented in a natural way or in a way that would mimic a real-world situation.
- **Adaptability**: Technology should be able to adapt to students' changing lives.

## Examples of Ubiquitous Learning

One example of ubiquitous learning is the use of computers and the internet to distribute **online courses** and **distance learning**. In the early days of distance learning, learning took place through mail. Instructors would mail assignments and course material to students and then students would mail complete work back to teachers. Later, with the invention of the internet, distance learning was conducted by using desktop computers and the internet. Now, distance learning isn't tied to typical places where desktop computers are located such as in a school or even a home office. Smartphones have enabled teachers and students to communicate with each other instantly.

## Advantages of Ubiquitous Learning

- **Learners can be anywhere**: Similar to previous implementations of learning using technology in education, learners are not tied to a certain location. However, because students often have their phones on them at all times, students have 24-7 access to a learning environment.
- **Saves time and money**: One of the most obvious advantages of u-learning is that you can save time and money. You can manage your schedule and take online courses at your most convenient time, whether early in the morning, late afternoon, or evening. You save money, too, because you don't have to pay for transportation or worry about eating on the go.
- **Better retention**: U-learning makes use of different platforms like Pedagogue, which provides interactive content. Also, you can share your thoughts and opinions with others. The more engaging the lessons, the more students can remember the information.

- **Personalized learning**: You can choose your learning path and study at your own pace. You become more motivated and invested in the course.
- **Cost-effective**: Students aren't the only ones that can save money in u-learning. Many educational institutions save money through this set-up because there's no need to use a physical classroom, which translates to reduced monetary spending.
- **Environment-friendly**: U-learning is also more environmentally friendly because it doesn't contribute to the pollution brought about by paper production.

## Disadvantages of U-learning

- **Lacks social interaction**: U-learning is one of the causes of social isolation because you don't see your teachers and classmates face-to-face anymore. Interaction is very limited to none.
- **Inaccessible to others**: Consider yourself lucky if you're located in an area where the internet connection is fast and stable. Unfortunately, some have very limited access to the internet. They have to go to internet cafes or use public Wi-Fis which is very inconvenient.
- **Cheating is unavoidable**: U-learning includes assessment, just like in a regular classroom setting. However, there are no teachers or proctors to watch over you during exams. It's easy for online students to share answers knowing there's nobody watching.
- **Requires self-motivation and proper time management skills**: You're basically on your own in u-learning. You have to motivate yourself to study hard, take down notes, and gather more information. You should also manage your time well by learning how to juggle studying while doing other things like household chores or earning money part-time.
- **Focuses more on theory**: You'll spend most of your time listening to podcasts, watching videos, and looking at slide presentations. There's no hand-on experience like conducting experiments.

# CONCEPT MAPPING

The concept mapping technique was developed by Joseph D. Novak at Cornell University. ′ Novak concluded that "Meaningful learning involves the assimilation of new concepts and propositions into existing cognitive structures". Novak's work was based on the theories of Ausubel. ′ Novak and Gowan (1984) have developed a theory of instruction that is based on Ausubel's meaningful learning principles that incorporates "concept maps" to represent meaningful relationships between concepts and propositions. Corbett, 2004 ′ A cognitive map is a "kind of visual road map showing some of the pathways we may take to connect meanings of concepts." According to Novak and Gowan, concept maps should be hierarchical. ′The more general, more inclusive concepts should be at the top of the map, and the more specific, less inclusive concepts at the bottom of the map. [Corbett, 2004]

## What is concept mapping?

Concept mapping is a technique for representing knowledge in graphs. Knowledge graphs are networks of concepts. Networks consist of nodes and links. Nodes represent concepts and links represent the relations between concepts. [Corbett, 2004] Concepts and links are labelled. Links can be unidirectional or bi-directional. Concepts and links may be categorized. They can be simply associative, Specified, or divided in categories such as causal or temporal relations. A concept map is a graphical representation of a person's (student's) knowledge of a domain. (Alpert & Grueneberg, 2001). The arrangement of major concepts from a text or lecture into a visual arrangement. Lines are drawn between associated concepts, and relationships between the connected concepts are named. These concept maps reveal the structural pattern in the material and provide the big picture. (Ehrlich, 2006)

**Purposes of Concept Mapping**: Plotnick (1997) lists five purposes of concept mapping: to generate ideas (brain storming, etc.) to design a complex structure (long texts, hypermedia, large web sites, etc.) to communicate complex ideas to aid learning by explicitly integrating new and old knowledge to assess understanding or diagnose misunderstanding

**Concept Mapping in Education:** Rationales for concept mapping in education are based on several connected ideas:

- General writing-to-learn arguments like writing favours making connections, or writing in a different genre favours meta-cognitive activities.
- Concept maps can prepare writing, assist in exploration and reading and be used as planning tools.
- More precisely: concept maps can be used as a creativity / brainstorming tool, as note taking tool, as planning tool for writing (in particular hypertexts) or project (e.g. conjecture map), as tool to express and communicate complex ideas.
- Concept maps could an assessment tool for the teacher and/or could be used as teaching materials.

**Types of Concept Maps:** Four major categories of concept maps are as under:

- **"Spider":** Organized by placing the central theme or unifying factor in the centre of the map. Outwardly radiating sub-themes surround the centre of the map.
- **"Flowchart":** Organizes information in a linear format.
- **"Hierarchical":** Presents information in a descending order of importance. The most important information is placed on the top. Distinguishing factors determine the placement of the information.
- **"Systems":** Organizes information in a format which is similar to a flowchart with the addition of 'inputs' and 'outputs'.

## Examples of Concept Maps

Students need to producing maps; the more they do it, the better they'll understand the process; viz.

- Begin with a simple topic, using a small number of concepts. Work through example(s) with the group, modifying the map where necessary – using post-it notes can help to develop confidence and facilitates changes. Emphasize importance of thinking about all possible links.
- Emphasize importance of writing down the nature of the links. Emphasize that there is no single "correct" answer; often more than one appropriate link.

- Emphasize importance of using arrows and their direction in describing the proposition.

The unique importance of mind mapping and concept mapping is really conferred with educational system. In the curriculum, educators follow concept and mind mapping for uplifting comprehension and learners can go beyond horizon. By a simple frame of mind and concept mapping teaching- learning can me made so easy. The peculiarity of maps maintains retention. A macro second is more than enough for reminding the concept using these modern educational practices. So, it is concluded that mind and concept maps are significant in the curriculum and both the educator and learner are benefitted with this.

## MIND MAPPING

The teaching learning process has to evolve into new face as the decades pass by and the modern instructional approaches are advancing for the same. The educational research follows a unique path in updating the pedagogy. So many approaches have been emerged out for making teaching learning easier. Mind map and concept maps are significant among them.

A mind map is a diagram used to visually organize information. A mind map is often created around a single concept, drawn as an image in the centre of a blank landscape page, to which associated representations of ideas such as images, words and parts of words are added. Mind Maps are a unique thinking tool that will bring out your natural genius and enable you to shine in every area of your life. Mind maps have following outcomes:

- Come up with innovative ideas and creative solutions
- Memorize information and recall it under pressure
- Set goals and achieve them
- Change career or start up your own venture
- Be an excellent time manager
- Run meetings with efficiency and ease
- Budget and plan to perfection
- Deliver excellent presentations with confidence
- Have more time for yourself and your family
- 10.Enjoy success after success in your life

**Origin:** The term "mind map" was first popularized by British popular psychology author and television personality Tony Buzan. The use of diagrams that visually "map" information using branching and radial maps traces back centuries. These pictorial methods record knowledge and model systems, and have a long history in learning, brainstorming, memory, visual thinking, and problem solving by educators, engineers, psychologists, and others.

**The process for creating a mind map can be described in eight steps:**

- **Step 1**: **Centre first:** Mind mapping begins with a word or image that symbolizes what you want to think about placed in the middle of the page. Centre first Step.
- **Step 2: Lighten up:** Start with an open, creative attitude. Let go of the idea of solving the entire problem, or writing a report that everyone will love. This is simply a brain dumping process that helps stimulate new ideas and connections. Centre first Lighten up.
- **Step 3 Free Associate:** Put down all ideas without judgement or evaluation. As ideas emerge, write one- or two-word descriptions of ideas on lines branching from the central focus. Allow the ideas to expand outward into branches and sub-branches. Centre first Lighten up Add branches
- **Step 4**: **Think fast:** Your brain works best in five-to-seven-minute bursts, so capture the ideas as rapidly as possible. Keywords, symbols and images provide a mental shorthand for recording ideas as quickly as possible. Centre first Lighten up Add branches Capture explosion of ideas Think fast
- **Step 5**: **Break boundaries:** The bigger the paper, the more ideas you'll have. Use different colours and styles. Break boundaries
- **Step 6**: **Don't judge:** Put everything down that comes to mind even if it is completely unrelated. If you're brainstorming ideas for a report on the status of carrots in Texas and you suddenly remember you need to pick-up your cleaning, put down "cleaning." Otherwise, your mind will get stuck like a record in that "cleaning" groove and you'll never generate those great ideas. Don't judge Don't judge Even unrelated

- **Step 7**: **Keep moving:** Keep your hand moving. If ideas slow down, draw empty lines, and watch your brain automatically find ideas to put on them. Centre first Think fast Don't judge Free associate Lighten up Add branches Break boundaries Keep moving.
- **Step 8**: **Allow organization:** Sometimes, you see relationships and connections immediately and you can add sub-branches to a main idea. Sometimes you don't, so you just connect the ideas to the central focus. Organization can always come later; the first requirement is to get the ideas out of your head and onto the paper.

The main benefits of using Mind Maps are (a) The process of creating a mind map is more interesting and entertaining than a standard chart or table. (b) Their visual quality permits users to highlight and review key points easily and more quickly than with standard sets of notes. (c) They facilitate recall, because the association of ideas, mirrors the way the brain works. (d) They help groups make sense out of things and help establish priorities.

**Mind Mapping vs Concept Mapping:** Concept maps - Mind maps differ from concept maps. Mind maps focus on only one word or idea, whereas concept maps connect multiple words or ideas. Also, concept maps typically have text labels on their connecting lines/arms. Mind maps are based on tree structures denoting relationships with a central governing concept, whereas concept maps are based on con

## A Brief History of Concept Mapping

Concept mapping is a technique for visualizing the relationships among different concepts. A concept map is a diagram showing the relationships among concepts. Concepts are connected with labelled arrows. The relationship between concepts is articulated in linking phrases, e.g., "gives rise to", "results in", "is required by," or "contributes to". It has subsequently been used as a tool to increase meaningful learning in the sciences and other subjects as well as to represent the expert knowledge of individuals and teams in education. Concept maps have their origin in the learning movement called constructivism. In particular, constructivists hold that learners actively construct knowledge. Novak's work is based on the cognitive theories, who stressed the importance of prior knowledge in being able to learn new concepts. "The most important single factor influencing learning is what the learner already knows. Ascertain this and teach accordingly."

## MODELS OF TEACHING

According to **Joyce and Weil (1985)**, a model of teaching is a plan or pattern that can be used to shape curricula, to design instructional materials and to guide instruction in the classroom and other setting. They describe the process of specifying and producing particular environment situations which cause the student to interact in such a way that specific change occurs in his behaviour.

### Characteristics of Models of Teaching

- **Scientific Procedure** - All models of teaching describe in detail the systematic steps to be followed. A model of teaching is not a haphazard combination of facts but on the other hand, it is of learners. They are based on certain assumptions.
- **Specification of certain Learning Outcomes** - All models of teaching specify the learning outcomes in detail on observable student's performance what the student will perform after completing an instructional sequence is specified in detail.
- **Specification of Environment -** This means that every model of teaching specifies in definite terms the environmental conditions under which student's response should be observed.
- **Certain Performance** - A model specified the criteria of **acceptable performance which is expected from the students**. The models of teaching delineate the behavioural outcomes which the learner would demonstrate after completing specific instructional sequence.
- **Specification of Operations** - All models of teaching specify mechanisms that provide for student reaction and interpretation with the environment.

### Functions

- Help in bringing about desirable changes in the behaviour of learners
- Help in achieving desirable teacher-pupil interaction during teaching

- Help in the construction of a curriculum or content of a course
- Useful to develop social efficiency, personal abilities, cognitive abilities and behavioural aspects of the student
- Help in designing appropriate educational activities
- Help in guiding the teacher to select appropriate teaching techniques, strategies and methods
- Help in the formation of a theory of teaching

**Elements/ Components:** Five major components are included in all teaching models. Each of these components will vary with the models. The five major components are;

- Focus
- Syntax
- Social system
- Principles of reaction
- Support system

Two **effects** can gain through the practise of a model; 1. Instructional effect, 2. Nurturant effect. The **Syntax** is the sequence of steps involved in the organization of the complete programme of teaching. The phases involved in the different models will differ. The **Social system** is the relationship between the teacher and the learners as well as the role played by each in the activities that take place. The **principles of reaction** are the nature of reaction expected from the teacher to every pupil activity. It gives guidance to the teacher as to how he is expected to react to each activity of the learners, to suit the characteristics of the model selected. The **Support system** is the Additional requirements other than the usual human skills or capacities of the teacher. The facilities usually available in the classroom. A description of this support system in advance will help the teacher ensure that he can apply the model successfully. The **Instructional Effects** are the **Direct Effects**, i.e. Effects of a lesson as purposefully envisaged by the teacher. The **Nurturant Effects** are the Indirect effects or Effects that might happen as a by-product.

## Families of Models of Teaching, Modern Models of Teaching

The term model is used to mean a teaching episode done by an experienced teacher in which a highly focussed teaching behaviour is demonstrated, in it an individual demonstrating particular patterns which the trainee learns through imitation. It is a way to talk and think about instruction in which certain facts may be organized, classified and interpreted. The classic definition of teaching is the design and creation of environments. Students learn by interacting with those environments and they study how to learn (Dewey, 1916). A model of teaching can be defined as the depiction of teaching and learning environment, including the behaviour of teachers and students while the lesson is presented through that model. Models of teaching enable the students to engage in robust cognitive and social task and teach the student how to use them productively. Models of teaching are the specific instructional plans which are designed according to the concerned learning theories. It provides a comprehensive blue print for curriculum to design instructional materials, planning lessons, teacher pupil roles, supporting aids and so forth.

Bruce Joyce and Marsha Weil (1972) describe a Model of Teaching as a plan or pattern that can be used to shape curricula, to design instructional materials and to guide instruction in the classroom and other settings. Thus, teaching models are just instructional designs. They describe the process and producing particular environmental situations which cause the student to interact in such a way that specific change occurs in his behaviour. Allen and Ryan (1969); Modelling is an individual demonstrating particular pattern which the trainee through imitation. B. K. Passi L. C. Singh and D. N. Sansanwal (1991); A model of teaching consist of guidelines for designing educational activities and environments. Model of teaching is a plan that can also be utilized to shape courses of studies, to design instructional material and to guide instruction.

According to N.K. Jangira and Azit Singh (1983): "A model of teaching is a set of inter-related components arranged in a sequence which provides guidelines to realize specific goal. It helps in designing instructional activities and environmental facilities, carrying out of these activities and realization of the stipulated objectives." Models of Teaching are designed for specific purposes-the teaching of information concepts, ways of thinking, the study of social values and so on-by asking students to engage in particular cognitive and social tasks. Some models centre on delivery by the instructor while others develop as the learners respond to tasks and the student is regarded as a partner in the educational enterprise.

## THE SUCHMAN INQUIRY MODEL

When children are young the world to them is full of questions to ask. Somewhere along the way, they get the idea that becoming an adult means leaving the world of questioning to enter the world of knowing the answers. Schools tend to encourage the movement from questions to answers since success becomes putting the right answer in the blank or marking the correct response. Questions in school tend to have one right answer and questions for which there are no answers are rare. It has been stated that true wisdom might best be defined as knowing how little one knows in contrast to how much one knows. Therefore, if knowing how to learn is more important than knowing all the answers, then one must realize that good questions are more important than right answers. Teaching students to question and ask quality questions is more important than the correctness of the answers they can give.

Teaching science through inquiry requires that students ask questions and figure things out for themselves. It involves the attempt to answer questions and seek information. Inquiry can be conducted in a variety of ways: observing nature, predicting outcomes, manipulating variables, analysing situations, and verifying assertions. It may involve discussing topics with others, reading, conducting field studies, surveys, and laboratory investigations, or all of these as one attempts to discover new knowledge and to figure things out. The inquiry model, developed by Richard Suchman, is based on the premise that the intellectual strategies used by scientists to solve problems and inquire into the unknown can be taught to students. Using the natural curiosity of students, they can be trained and disciplined in the procedures of inquiry. The model was developed from analysing the methods used in creative research personnel. The elements of their inquiry process were identified and these were built into an instructional model called inquiry training. Inquiry training is designed to bring students directly into the scientific process through exercises that compress the scientific process into small periods of time. The training has resulted in an increased understanding of subject, more creative thinking, and skills for obtaining and analysing information and students can establish facts, build concepts, and then generate and test explanations or theories. The students are active learners involved in exploration, questioning, problem solving, inductive reasoning, invention, labelling, and discovery. The inquiry process will help students:

- Approach future problems with confidence in their abilities to seek out the solution
- To begin to consider success and failure as information rather than reward or punishment
- Practice the process to develop the ability to sense the relevance of variables, make intuitive leaps, and put problems into forms with which they know how to work
- Improve their memory process because when they integrate material into their own cognitive structure, thus material is made more readily retrievable

The inquiry training method requires active participation in scientific inquiry and capitalizes on the student's natural curiosity. The general goals of inquiry training are to:

- Develop the intellectual discipline and skills necessary to raise questions and search out answers stemming from their natural curiosity.
- Acquire and process data logically.
- Develop intellectual strategies that they can use to find out why things are as they are.

The Inquiry Training Model is based on Suchman's theory that:

- Students inquire naturally when they are puzzled.
- They can become conscious of and learn to analyse their thinking strategies.
- New strategies can be taught directly and added to the students existing ones.
- Cooperative inquiry enriches thinking and helps students to learn about the tentative, emergent nature of knowledge and to appreciate alternative explanations.

This model differs from other inquiry models in the way the data are presented. Students gather data in a simulated process through questioning rather than actual manipulation of data. Thus, the method is more process oriented as the primary goal is to improve students' ability to relate data to the inferences they have formed. The Inquiry training has five phases.

- The first phase is the student's confrontation with the puzzling situation.
- Phases two and three are the date gathering and operations of verification and experimentation. In the data-gathering phases, the students ask a series of question that the teacher answers with a yes or no, and they conduct a series of experiments of the problem situation.
- In the fourth phase, the students organize the information obtained during the data-gathering phases and try to explain the discrepancy.
- In the last phase, students analyse the problem-solving strategies they used during the inquiry. The teacher's role is to construct the problem situation, to referee the inquiry procedures, to respond to students' inquiry probes with the necessary information, to help students establish a focus in there, and to facilitate discussion of the problem situation among the students.

## Presentation of the model

Preparation for the Inquiry: Identify a problem requiring an explanation. In selecting the problem or event, these criteria need to be considered. The event must pose a problem which requires a discoverable explanation, as opposed to teaching a fact, concept, or generalization. The problem must be genuinely interesting and stimulating to the learner. The level of the problem must be approximately matched with the level of the learner. The curiosity and motivation of the student are enhanced if the problem is prepared in a way which makes it appear discrepant. The event focuses the student on a particular problem rather than on a set of problems in general. In selecting the medium for presenting the problem/event, design experiences which will bring students into contact with a problem-evoking situation. Discrepant events, demonstrations, films, audio tapes, graphs, tables, problems and case studies can be used to start the inquiry process. It must be a puzzling situation to the students and conflict with the idea of reality. The model can be presented in a variety of ways. To help the students improve their thinking skills, have them work in groups and follow the format on the worksheet.

### Inquiry Training Lesson

**Phase One: Confrontation with the Problem:** Present the problem situation. Explain the inquiry procedures to the students. They are to gather data through questions they ask of the teacher/ instructor who will be the main source of data. Each question must be asked as tentative hypothesis. The questions should obey two criteria: they must be answerable yes or no. (This places the responsibility for analysing the problem on the students.) And the results must be obtainable through observations rather than requiring an inference. The teacher may decide to add information or expand on the problem at any time; however, it is important that students experience some frustration as they question. Instead of asking students, "Is this what you mean?" it is better to say, "Can you repeat the question?" or "Can you state the question so I can answer is yes or no?" Avoid answering the questions for them. A teacher might say, "Yes, that is part of the answer, but why don't you consider this additional piece of information in light of what you have already discovered." Once called on, the student may ask as many questions as he/she wishes before yielding the floor to another student. Students must understand that they may ask question only when called upon. Students should be encouraged to work together whenever possible. Encourage the students to call for a caucus when they need to talk to each other, but do not permit them to talk to each other during the questioning periods.

**Phase Two: Data Gathering—Verification:** Gather information about the event/problem to verify the nature of the objects and conditions. Confirm the occurrence of the problem situation. The data should be recorded on the board or on data sheets kept by each student.

**Phase Three: Data Gathering – Experimentation:** Isolate relevant variables. Students introduce new elements into the situation to see if the even happens differently, changing things to see what will happen. Students hypothesize a solution to the problem. When a student poses a theoretical question that seems to be an answer to the problem, the question is stated as a theory and written on the board. Now all data gathering is related directly to proving or disproving this theory. Students may caucus to discuss the information and nature of the problem and frame hypothetical questions which they will ask of the instructor. Depending on the nature of the problem, the students could be directed to other sources of information, activities, or to actual experimentation in the laboratory. They can also use a series of questions of the teacher to test the hypothesis. Hypothesis are confirmed or revised. If the theory seems verified, then the class accepts the hypothesis as a solution and moves to the next step. If the hypothesis is not acceptable and is rejected by the class, then general data gathering begins again. Another hypothesis may be posed and tested until a hypothesis has been accepted by the group.

**Phase Four: Organizing, Formulating an Explanation:** Ask the students to explain the hypothesis that has been accepted as a tentative solution to the problem and organize the data to support the hypothesis. They should determine how the hypothesis could be tested to see if the date can be generalized to other situations. When the students state their explanation so we can measure the range of the possibilities are noted.

**Phase Five: Analysis of the Inquiry Process**: a. Ask the students to review the process they have just used to arrive at acceptance of the hypothesis (their pattern of inquiry). Which questions were the most effective? Which direction of questioning was the most productive? Which questions were not helpful? What type of information was needed and not obtained? b. Discuss ways that they could have improved their inquiry.

## CURRICULUM DEVELOPMENT

According to John Kerr, a curriculum is planned and guided by the school, whether it is carried on in groups, individually inside or outside the school. Curriculum development describes all the ways in which teaching or training organization plans and guides learning. This learning can take place in groups or with individual learners. It can take place inside or outside the classroom. It can take place in an institutional setting like school, college, training centre, or in a village or a field. It is central to the teaching-learning process.

### Activities involved in Curriculum development

- conceptualizing the curriculum,

- selecting and organizing the content, material and learning experiences
- suggesting the method and ways of providing these experiences
- Evaluating the learning outcomes in terms of attainment of desired educational objectives.
- Need and importance of curriculum development (or construction)
- Curriculum development is a purposeful activity.
- It is undertaken to design or redesign for the realization of certain specific educational objectives.
- The curriculum is the heart of the student's college/school experience.
- The curriculum should be reviewed and revised on a regular basis so that it is able to serve the changing needs of both students and society.

## Principles of curriculum development

- Suitability to the age and mental level of the children
- According to the specific interests of students
- The curriculum should be environmentally centred
- The principle of the comprehensive curriculum
- Principle of co-relation
- The principle of practical work
- Principle of flexibility
- Principle of forward-looking
- The principle of consultation with teachers
- The principle of the joint venture
- The principle of availability of time and other resources

## Curriculum Organization

Process of selecting curriculum elements form the subject, the current social life and the students experience then designing the selected curriculum elements appropriately so thy they can form the curriculum structure and type.

## Patterns of Curriculum Organization

- Subject Centred Pattern of Curriculum:
- Student Centred Pattern of Curriculum:
- Activity/Experience Centred Pattern of Curriculum:
- The Broad Fields Curriculum Design:
- Correlated Pattern of Curriculum:
- Integrated Pattern of Curriculum:
- Core Pattern of Curriculum:

## Models of Curriculum Development

Curriculum theory is a set of related educational concepts that affords a systematic and illumination g perspective of curriculum phenomena. Focusing on the historical and the conceptual roots of curriculum theory approaches, the argument is that the dispute and the separation between normative and critical roles of curriculum theories are important to overcome in today's competency-based and outcome-focused context of higher education. It is suggested that in the debate between normative and critical curriculum approaches, a danger is that the focus on the educational importance of curricula may be neglected and silenced in the midst of the pressure to renew curricula in higher education.

"Evaluation is the collection of, analysis and interpretation of information about any aspect of a programme of education or training as part of a recognized process of judging its effectiveness, its efficiency and any other outcomes it may have." Evaluation is a systematic determination of a subject's merit, worth and significance, using criteria governed by a set of standards. The primary purpose of evaluation, in addition to gaining insight into prior or existing initiatives, is to enable reflection and assist in the identification of future change. Evaluation is the structured interpretation and giving of meaning to predict or actual impacts of proposals or results. It looks at original objectives, and at what are either predicted or what was accomplished and how it was accomplished. So, evaluation can be formative that is taking place during the development of a concept or proposal, project or organization, with the intention of improving the value or effectiveness of the proposal, project, or organization. It can also be summative, drawing lessons from a completed action or project or an organization at a later point in time or circumstance. Evaluations are normally divided into two categories: Formative and Summative.

A **formative evaluation** (sometimes referred to as internal) is a method for judging the worth of a program while the program activities are forming (in progress). They can be conducted during any phase of the teaching learning process. This part of the evaluation focuses on the process. In this evaluation the proper learning interventions can take place that allows the learners to master the required skills and knowledge. A **summative evaluation** (sometimes referred to as external) is a method of judging the worth of a program at the end of the program activities (summation). The focus is on the outcome. The various instruments used to collect the data are questionnaires, surveys, interviews, observations, and testing. The model or methodology used to gather the data should be a specified step-by-step procedure. It should be carefully designed and executed to ensure the data is accurate and valid.

**Evaluation Instrument**: An evaluation instrument as something that an Internet user could use to assess the quality of a website containing health information. Instruments were selected if they provided the user with explicit instructions for evaluating the quality of a website containing health information.

**Different types of assessments:** By using different types of assessment, we can understand student progress in various ways and adapt your teaching strategies accordingly. The various types of assessments are:

- Diagnostic assessments.
- Formative assessments.
- Summative assessments.
- Impassive assessments.
- Norm-referenced assessments.
- Criterion-referenced assessments

## BLOOM'S TAXONOMY

Bloom's Taxonomy comprises three learning domains: the cognitive, affective, and psychomotor, and assigns to each of these domains a hierarchy that corresponds to different levels of learning. It's important to note that the different levels of thinking defined within each domain of the Taxonomy are hierarchical.

## Blooms Revised taxonomy

There are six levels of cognitive learning according to the revised version of Bloom's Taxonomy. Each level is conceptually different. The six levels are remembering, understanding, applying, analysing, evaluating, and creating.

- **Remember**: Definition: retrieve, recall, or recognize relevant knowledge from long-term memory. Appropriate learning outcome verbs for this level include: cite, define, describe, identify, label, list, match, name, outline, quote, recall, report, reproduce, retrieve, show, state, tabulate, and tell.
- **Understand**: Definition: demonstrate comprehension through one or more forms of explanation Appropriate learning outcome verbs for this level include: abstract, arrange, articulate, associate, categorize, clarify, classify, compare, compute, conclude, contrast, defend, diagram, differentiate, discuss, distinguish, estimate, exemplify, explain, extend, extrapolate, generalize, give examples of, illustrate, infer, interpolate, interpret, match, outline, paraphrase, predict, rearrange, reorder, rephrase, represent, restate, summarize, transform, and translate.
- **Apply**: Definition: use information or a skill in a new situation Appropriate learning outcome verb for this level include: apply, calculate, carry out, classify, complete, compute, demonstrate, dramatize, employ, examine, execute, experiment, generalize, illustrate, implement, infer, interpret, manipulate, modify, operate, organize, outline, predict, solve, transfer, translate, and use.
- **Analyse**: Definition: break material into its constituent parts and determine how the parts relate to one another and/or to an overall structure or purpose Appropriate learning outcome verbs for this level include: analyse, arrange, break down, categorize, classify, compare, connect, contrast, deconstruct, detect, diagram, differentiate, discriminate, distinguish,

divide, explain, identify, integrate, inventory, order, organize, relate, separate, and structure.

- **Evaluate**: Definition: make judgments based on criteria and Appropriate learning outcome verbs for this level include: appraise, apprise, argue, assess, compare, conclude, consider, contrast, convince, criticize, critique, decide, determine, discriminate, evaluate, grade, judge, justify, measure, rank, rate, recommend, review, score, select, standardize, support, test, and validate.
- **Create**: Definitions: put elements together to form a new coherent or functional whole; reorganize elements into a new pattern or structure. Appropriate learning outcome verbs for this level include: arrange, assemble, build, collect, combine, compile, compose, constitute, construct, create, design, develop, devise, formulate, generate, hypothesize, integrate, invent, make, manage, modify, organize, perform, plan, prepare, produce, propose, rearrange, reconstruct, reorganize, revise, rewrite, specify, synthesize, and write.

## Harrow's Taxonomy

Anita Harrow's taxonomy for the psychomotor domain is organized according to the degree of coordination including involuntary responses as well as learned capabilities. Simple reflexes begin at the lowest level of the taxonomy, while complex neuromuscular coordination makes up the highest levels.

- **Reflex movements:** The actions elicited without learning in response to some stimuli. Examples include: flexion, extension, stretch, postural adjustments.
- **Basic fundamental movement:** An inherent movement pattern which is formed by combining of reflex movements and is the basis for complex skilled movements. Examples are: walking, running, pushing, twisting, gripping, grasping, manipulating.
- **Perceptual**: Refers to interpretation of various stimuli that enable one to make adjustments to the environment. Visual, auditory, kinaesthetic, or tactile discrimination. Suggests cognitive as well as psychomotor behaviour. Examples

include: coordinated movements such as jumping rope, punting, or catching.

- **Physical activities:** It requires endurance, strength, vigour, and agility which produce a sound, efficiently functioning body. Examples are: all activities which require a) strenuous effort for long periods of time; b) muscular exertion; c) a quick, wide range of motion at the hip joints; and d) quick, precise movements.
- **Skilled movements:** The result of the acquisition of a degree of efficiency when performing a complex task. Examples are: all skilled activities obvious in sports, recreation, and dance.
- **Non-discursive communication:** The communication through bodily movements ranging from facial expressions through sophisticated choreographic. Examples include: body postures, gestures, and facial expressions efficiently executed in skilled dance movement and choreographic.

## STANDARDIZED ACHIEVEMENT TEST

Standardized tests are designed to show a student's skills and abilities at a given point in his or her schooling in relation to other children of the same age in schools across the state and the nation. Steps in the achievement test are (a) Planning, (b) Construction, (c) Evaluation, and (d) Validation.

**Reliability and validity:** Reliability and validity are the concepts used to evaluate the quality of research. They indicate how well a method, technique or test measure something. Reliability is about the consistency of a measure, and validity is about the accuracy of a measure. Reliability is a measure of the stability or consistency of test scores. Reliability refers to the extent that the instrument yields the same results over multiple trials. Validity refers to the extent that the instrument measures what it was designed to measure. Construct validity uses statistical analyses, such as correlations, to verify the relevance of the questions. The tricky part is that a test can be reliable without being valid. However, a test cannot be valid unless it is reliable. An assessment can provide us with consistent results, making it reliable, but unless it is measuring what we are supposed to measure, it is not valid.

**Norm referenced tests:** It measures the acquisition of skills and knowledge from multiple sources such as notes, texts and syllabi. A norm-referenced test is a type of test, assessment, or evaluation which yields an estimate of the position of the tested individual in a predefined population, with respect to the trait being measured. The term normative assessment refers to the process of comparing one test-taker to his or her peers.

**Criterion referenced tests**: It measures performance on specific concepts and are often used in a pre-test / post-test format. Criterion-referenced tests focus on "what test takers can do and what they know, not how they compare to others"

**Question Banks:** It allows us to create, preview, and edit stored questions. Question banks can store questions within categories. The categories can be limited to being used on the site, course, or quiz level. The questions stored in the question bank can be reused in different quizzes and lessons. Questions-Bank means that each question has a weight and area of knowledge deals with it. The system facilitates generation of automatic, balanced, and different exam sheets, that containing different types of questions, covering the entire curriculum, and displaying gradually from easiness to difficulty.

**Open Book Examination:** An "open book examination" is that in which students are allowed to refer to class notes and summaries or a "memory aid", textbooks, or other approved material while answering questions. It's like question paper is given to students prior to sitting the formal exam or are to complete as a 'take-home' exam. "Open-book exams allow students to take notes, texts or resource materials into an exam situation. They test their ability to find and apply information and knowledge, so are often used in subjects requiring direct reference to written materials, like law statutes, statistics or acts of parliament.

## INSTRUCTIONAL DESIGN

During the 2nd World War, a considerable amount of training materials for the military were developed based on the principles of instruction, learning and human behaviour. Tests for assessing a learner's abilities were used to screen candidates in the army. After the success of military training, psychologists began to view training as a system, and developed various analysis, design and evaluation procedures. In other words, the birth of instructional design is strongly reflected on one hand to the emergence of empirical research in psychology and education and on the other to specific needs of the system.

**What is Instructional Design?** Instructional Design is the systematic process of translating general principles of learning and instruction into plans for instructional materials and activities. Instructional Design is defined as "a systematic process that is employed to develop education and training program in a consistent and reliable fashion. "(Reiser & Dempsy, 2007). Instructional design is that branch of knowledge concerned with theory and practice, related to instructional strategies and systematic procedures for developing and implementing those strategies.

## How to design instructions?

Learning has three domains- cognitive (learning involves thinking like thinking about the key that can open the lock, or why cactus grows in desert); affective (learning involves feelings and we learn to respect our environment, wild life; empathize with the underprivileged; appreciate honesty); and psychomotor (learning involves coordination of thought and physical movement like carpentry, handling lab equipment, administering an injection, and so on). You need to teach for making learners think/ develop right attitude / perform tasks involving thought and movements. While designing instructions we need to consider for which domain(s) of learning we are going to develop courseware. Further, for the three domains of learning Gagne described five capabilities that learning should develop. These are: Intellectual Skills (like that used for solving problems, understanding concepts, etc.), Cognitive Strategy (ability to monitor own learning, and track one's progress), Verbal Information (such as being able to describe something); Attitude (like respect for wildlife), Motor Skills (like dancing, skating, administering injection, etc.). Gagne however says that instructions should not aim to develop any one/few of these but must have multiple aims and learners need to attain several varieties of learned capabilities. After setting instructional goals, the next step is to design instructions for attaining the goals. Gagne described nine events for designing Instructional Design. These instructional events and the corresponding learning processes provide a general framework (structure) along which you can design instructions in the following way:

- Gain attention: you can use techniques like asking questions to arouse curiosity, describing an event that creates interest in the topic, and so on for drawing your learners' attention.
- Inform learners the objectives (purpose) to make them interested in the topic.
- Stimulate recall of prior learning experiences for attaching new ones to it.
- Present the content in a meaningful way, and provide necessary explanations and examples so that learning is meaningful.
- Provide learning guidance in the form of examples, glossary, cases, summary, and the like.
- Elicit performance by including activities that provide scope for practice.
- Provide feedback on learners' performances.
- Assess performance by checking learning outcomes against instructional objectives through assignments, tests, and the like.
- Enhance retention and transfer of learning by providing cues and strategies of retrieval of learning call of prior learning experiences for attaching new ones to it.

## Steps for developing Instructional Design

Instructional Design model: typically specified method, that is followed will facilitate the transfer of knowledge, skills and attitude to the recipient or acquirer of the instruction. Instructional Design is the systematic development of instructional specifications using learning and instructional theory to ensure the quality of instruction. It is the entire process of analysis of learning needs and goals and the development of a delivery system to meet those needs. It includes development of instructional materials and activities; and try out and evaluation of all instruction and learner activities.

## Role of Instructional Design

- Systematic process of Instructional Design enables you to:
- Identify performance a problem

- Determine the goals and objectives
- Define your learners and their needs.
- Develop strategies to meet needs and goals.
- Evaluate goods, objectives, and needs are met.

Instructional Design Approach ensures:

- There is a need for training.
- The learning events are well – designed.
- Quality training materials are developed.
- Learning events are implemented using appropriate strategies or approaches.
- Learning events are evaluated to ensure that learning has taken place.

## Purpose of Instructional Design

Instructional Design helps the teacher to develop her capacity to teach more students and create conductive environment for them. It helps curriculum makers to plan learning centre and curriculum which provides a variety of educational experience to students. It helps to make materials and create more interesting and effective instructional material and learning sources. It stimulates to develop the new educational forms and educational opportunities which will replace the schools of today.

## Advantages of Instructional Design:

- Support effective, efficient and appealing instruction.
- Facilitates congruence among objective, activities and assessment.
- Provides a systematic framework for dealing with learning problems,
- Learning effectiveness

## Disadvantages of Instructional Design:

- Instructional Design does not have limits of applicability, it is not the solution to all the ills and problems of education and training, nor is it the only method for creating education.

- Time consuming in a way that it takes times to learn how to follow the instructional design procedures and time to implement them when the training being created.
- A good instructional design requires a number of resources.

### Theoretical Foundations of Instructional Design

**Firstly**, Instructional Design theory is founded in learning theory, pedagogical theory and instructional theory and draws from many other fundamental disciplines such as motivation research. All these disciplines have their word to say about pedagogic strategy. **Second**, it's also a craft, i.e. an engineering discipline whose methods draw a lot from software engineering. **Third**, modern sophisticated instructional designs make use of educational designs make use of educational technologies. Some authors even argue that some of the more interesting designs cannot be done without technology. Instructional design and educational technology depend on each other. **Fourth**, the planning of a learning environment in the sense of instructional design should be evidence oriented. This means, that decisions for methods, design and motivation are accredited through empirical results. This can be reached through empirical results. This can be reached through design patterns, edit formats which have been approved to solve a problem (Niegemann, 2013).

## INSTRUCTIONAL DESIGN MODEL

It is typically specified method, that if followed will facilitate the transfer of knowledge, skills and attitude to the recipient or acquirer of the instruction. It is based on theory (learning theory, systems theory) or practice (company, military, and software development). It gives us structure and meaning to problem.

### Some Instructional Design Models

A teacher may follow a particular model of classroom management. City planners may use a model of urban planning. An engineer may use a particular model of high-rise apartments. We may model our behaviour as per the behaviour of our role model. There are also various models of running organisations, farming practices, and so on. A model is thus a particular way of carrying out a process, and there are various models for designing instructions. Some models of Instructional Design are as follows:

- ADDIE Model: it means Analysis, Design, Development, Implementation, Evaluation ADDIE is an acronym that covers the major processes of Instructional Design, which are - Analysis, Design, Development, Implementation, and Evaluation. Many models developed later are based on this model.
- Dick and Carey Model: This model does not treat its component as isolated parts but considers these as interrelated parts that influence each other and work as a system. It also considers context, and hence takes into account learners' (audience) profile including prior understanding so that instructions are provided to build upon the prior knowledge
- ASSURE Model: This model has the following steps: A – Analyse Learners- learners' needs and characteristics are examined. S – State Standards and Objectives for the instructions, specifying what learners will be able to do following the instruction. S – Select Strategies, Technology, Media, and Materials for imparting instructions. U – Utilise Technology, Media, and Materials- planning how to use technology, media, and materials. The content needs to be prepared/ procured, previewed and provided as learning experiences. R – Require Learner Participation- planning how learners will be engaged actively as a group and individually in learning. E – Evaluate and Revise- same as in ADDIE model
- ARCS: It means Attention, Relevance, Confidence, Satisfaction ARCS model The ARCS model describes strategies for stimulating and sustaining motivation for learning (Park, 2018) through the following steps: **Attention**: Need to draw learners' attention. You have read in this unit that attention is essential for learning. You have also read that strategies that create novelty or stimulate curiosity through questions, description of problematic situations and the like are useful for drawing learners' attention. Creating variation in instructional material also helps to sustain attention. The content of this unit is therefore interspersed with cases, information in boxes, and activities. **Relevance**: Learning

experience that are relevant or meaningful to learners and fulfil their learning needs, motivate them. One way to establish the relevance of the learning materials is to use authentic or real-world examples. For instance, in teacher education courses inclusion of problems commonly faced in schools makes the content relevant. **Confidence**: When instructions enhance the feeling of confidence and self-efficacy in learners, learners are motivated. Therefore, we need to take steps like including content that matches prior knowledge of learners, explaining the content well, using simple language and the like. **Satisfaction**: Satisfying outcomes motivate learners. Intrinsic motivation emerges from accomplishing tasks and feedback communicating this helps. Tasks selected for learners therefore should be doable and provision of feedback should be there.

- **Cognitive apprenticeship model**: This model is useful for teaching skills (psychomotor domain). It is based on Albert Bandura's theory of cognitive apprenticeship. As per this theory a skill is modelled, and learners need to be attentive, motivated, must have access to information and retain the information presented, and must be able to accurately reproduce the desired skill. You have read this in the earlier sections that knowledge can be constructed through observation. Hence, modelling behaviours /acts like an expert's dance steps, way of cooking, repairing machines and so on helps to learn these activities.

## Benefits of Instructional Design

- Serves the learning needs and success of students through effective presentation of content and fostering of interaction.
- Allow instructor to anticipate and meet potential concerns/ambiguities.
- May help ensure the quality of a course.
- Gives structure to the student's process of working through course material.

These instructional design models are integral to creating efficient, effective, appealing, engaging, and inspiring learning experiences across industries. The task of an instructional designer is to facilitate learning so that learners are able to apply their newly acquired knowledge, skills and attitudes in a range of situations. The systematic and sound application of learning theories and principles to produce functional learning materials fundamentally supports a learner-centred and outcomes-based approach. In this way learners are expected to demonstrate improved job performances or graduation rates. The main advantage of instructional systems design (ISD) is that it is a systematic decision-making process of finding a solution to an instructional problem. The ISD approach brings about innovations that can translate learning problems into instructional plans so that the quality of the instruction is assured. ISD focuses on achieving set learning outcomes and, therefore, the instructional objectives show all stakeholders (e.g., learners, learning facilitators, administrators, employers and parents) what the intentions of the learning materials are. Performance standards and assessment criteria provide a means of determining whether or not those outcomes have been met. Clients and users can thus trust the effectiveness of the instruction, because all aspects that would influence the design are considered and the final version of the learning materials has been revised and tried out until the learning outcomes are met. Instructional Designers utilize skills and knowledge in the areas of learning theory. The instructional process enabling technologies to facilitate the creation of effective instruction and learning environments.

## LAURILLARD'S CONVERSATIONAL MODEL

Teaching can be defined as a design science, where it uses what is known about teaching to achieve the objective of student learning by improving them with the implementation of designs. Hence, constant efforts are made by the researchers and teachers to achieve their learning outcome. Diana Laurillard is a Professor of Educational Technology and Pro-Vice Chancellor for Learning Technologies and Teaching at The Open University. Laurillard's conversational framework was developed to guide and provide what learners needed and to explore how best to support their learning (Laurillard, 2008). The traditional method of delivering education has got problems. However, with the advancement of technology, it is probable to find solutions for these problems. The Conversational Framework was developed by analysing the findings from research on student learning, and using these to generate the requirements of the teacher who is responsible for designing the learning process for their students (Laurillard, 2002).

The Laurillard's Conversional Model is a teaching strategy, designed to benefit the best from technology to the world of education. The framework highlights the necessity of conversation between teacher and student, over transmission of information from teacher to student. According to Laurillard, the acquisition of complicated concepts and the construction of conceptual distinctions are essential to much academic learning. The teacher's concepts, the teacher's constructed learning environment, the student's concepts, and the student's individual behaviours are regarded the four components for efficient learning. 'The Conversational Framework is a way of capturing the iterative, communicative, adaptive, reflective and goal□oriented actions with feedback that are necessary to support the complete learning process. '

According to this Framework, the learning process can be operated at two levels, namely, discursive and experimental. At Discursive level, exchange of theoretical ideas and concepts takes place between the teachers and students. This learning process is done through listening, reading, writing, discussing, communicating, presenting etc. Whereas, at the experimental level, teachers construct a learning environment and students are supposed to work in that environment bring out a practice output in exchange. Examples of such learning environment includes field trip, practice class, experimental labs etc. The whole framework is intended for teachers and students by carrying out activities of adaptation and reflection. With the given concepts, teachers adapt an appropriate task for the learners further reflect their performance at the experimental level to facilitate discussions and presentations at discursive level.

This framework is focused on the act of learning. It designed to help teachers to analyse whether the strategies that they have undertaken to teach their students are enough to achieve their learning outcomes. According to Laurillard, different media forms offer varying affordances or levels of support for distinct types of learning experiences. She distinguishes five different types of media: narrative, interactive, communicative, adaptive, and productive.

- "**Narrative** media tell or show the learner something," according to Conole and Fill (2005). (e.g. text, image).

- The learner's actions are only partially responded to by **interactive** media (e.g. search engines, multiple choice tests, simple models).
- People can **communicate** more easily with the help of communication medium (e.g. email, discussion forum).
- What the learner performs affects **adaptive** media (e.g. some simulations, virtual worlds).
- The student can use **productive** media to create anything (e.g., a word processor or a spreadsheet)."

The following table is from Peter Clinch (2005) will give more clarity towards the Laurillard's Conversional Model.

| learning experience | method/technologies | media forms |
|---|---|---|
| attending, apprehending | print, TV, video, DVD | narrative |
| investigating, exploring | library, CD, DVD, Web resources | interactive |
| discussing, debating | seminar, online conference | communicative |
| experimenting, practising | laboratory, field trip, simulation | adaptive |
| articulating, expressing | essay, product, animation, model | productive |

## Laurillard's Six Learning Types

1. **Acquisition:** Learners acquire knowledge through reading, watching videos and listening audios.
2. **Investigation:** Allowing learners to direct their learning and skill development is the goal of an investigation or inquiry. The learner's knowledge and comprehension are developed through activities that are closely related to the discipline's authentic practise. Learners investigate, compare, and evaluate concepts and ideas that are being taught or incorporated in training materials.
3. **Discussion:** Learners discuss in groups and forums, share experience in seminars etc. They also need to interact with others. Consider others' point of view and attempt to defend their own.
4. **Practice:** Learners practise a skill or knowledge by completing a practical assignment and using the feedback to better their next action. To help learners improve their next activity or future performance, you can combine and follow

this with offering feedback, incorporating peer feedback, or self-reflection. Learners discuss in groups and forums, share experience in seminars etc. They also need to interact with others. Consider others' point of view and attempt to defend their own. E.g. Role- play activities, virtual lab and field trips

5. **Collaboration:** Learners work together to build on each other's learning through joint practice and production as well as discussion and feedback. They gain knowledge by collaborating on a project or assignment. They create something to discover meaning, a solution to a problem, or to demonstrate what they've learned. Collaboration occurs throughout online or offline conversation, practise, and production and is based on research and acquisition.
6. **Production**: Learners apply what they've learned into practice. They consolidate their knowledge by producing tangible artefacts or communicating their present understanding and how they apply it in practice. E.g. Performing or presenting to an audience

The Laurillard's conversional framework is iterative goal-action-feedback cycle that help the learners to refine and develop ideas and conceptual understanding. The paradigm emphasises that rather than being pre-set in advance, these activities should be produced and altered based on the conceptual discourse. Finally, as part of the teaching and learning process, opportunities for reflection and feedback are provided, which can be difficult in big classes or lectures. Conversional framework is extremely challenging for the most used learning technologies such as podcast, webinar etc. To illustrate, after the outbreak of covid-19 a sudden swift to remote learning was tough to both teachers and students. It is not the access to materials or communication that quality of the learning experience provided, instead it depends on to what extent the learning process is fully supported. In order to support a complete learning process, they need to offer the students the following:

- a task goal;
- a working environment for the learner to practise their actions;
- meaningful feedback on their actions in relation to the goal;
- the opportunity to revise and improve their actions;

- the encouragement to adapt and reflect in the light of experience.

The Laurillard's conversional framework is an effective method to analyze and resolve the problems that has been existing in the current teaching strategies by facilitating a blend of technology and teaching.

## FIVE STAGE MODEL OF GILLY SALMON

A model of teaching consists of guidelines for designing educational activities and environments. It specifies ways of teaching and learning that are intended to achieve certain kind of goals (Weil and Joyce,1978). The most important aim of teaching model is to improve the instructional effectiveness in an interactive atmosphere and shape curriculum. It is useful in planning for systematic teaching. Models are prescriptive teaching strategies designed to accomplish particular instructional goals. Model of teaching is a blue print designed in advance for providing necessary structure and direction to the teacher for realizing the stipulated objectives. The teaching models are useful for teachers for planning and organizing teaching activities. The teacher can use this model in planning curriculum, designing student-teacher interaction and student activities and finally it may be helpful in formulating and developing theories of teaching

Dr Gilly Salmon, British e-learning specialist and professor. She has been a digital learning innovator for more than thirty years. Gilly Salmon born in Southend, Essex, England. She was the founder and CEO of Education Alchemist Ltd a company formed around her life work. She has been worked as Academic Director for Open Education Service (OEC), Prof. of innovation and transformation and Associate Dean at University of Liverpool and also hold the position as Pro-Vice Chancellor at University of Western Australia. She worked as Head of Beyond Distance Research Alliance and Media Zoo at University of Leicester in UK.

Prof Gilly Salmon is one of the world's leading thinkers in digital and blended learning. She researches and publishes widely in the themes of innovations and changes in Higher Education and exploitation of new technologies of all kinds in the service of learning. She is internationally renowned for her significant contributions to education futures including research, innovation, programme design, teaching methods and the use of new technologies. Dr. Gilly Salmon at present working as Academic Director at Online Education services (OES) in UK.

Dr Gilly Salmon developed a structured development process to make online learning to be successful and happy. The five-stage model provides a framework or a scaffold for a structured and paced programme of E-tivities. The five-stage model offers essential support and development to participants at each stage as they buildup expertise in learning online. Dr Gilly Salman's five stage model is an approach to e-learning, based on four factors:

- Design of curriculum and activities
- Pedagogy
- Role of Teacher (Facilitator)
- Technology

Dr Gilly's model consisted of five important pedagogical constructs. These constructs referred as the five stages of this model. They are entitled as below.

- **Individual access and motivation:** At this stage E-tivities are need to be designed carefully to enable the participants to find online platform. Participants might be nervous at this stage. E-tivities should be cordially invite the learners. The individual access and induction of participants into an online learning are essential prerequisites for online conference participation. Initially simple activities or icebreakers are used to enable the participants to become involved and feel comfortable with technology.
- **Online Socialization:** E-tivities at this stage enabling the participants to relate with few others. At this stage E-tivities promotes the establishment of a micro community through active and interactive activities. Individual participants establishing their own identities. Here the activities to be designed to provide practice, not in technology but in working together. This group interaction provides the important cultural context for learning and activate the process of knowledge construction.
- **Information Exchange:** In this context Etivities prioritizing content, enabling participants to impart information to each

other, explain and clarify. It also focused on exploring, coordination and communication between participants. Etivities at this stage also recommends for group working. Tutors facilitating structured activities. They assign roles and responsibilities to the participants.

- **Knowledge construction:** Learning communities adopts themselves to work online, managing their time and broadening the understanding ability. The participants move towards peer directed Etivities and team works They practicing a collaborative approach in order to expertise learning.
- **Development:** At this stage Dr Salman suggested E-tivities for gaining self-insight and making judgment on experience. The participants became potential for evaluating, critical thinking, demonstration, meta cognitive awareness and judgment.

**Graphical Representation of five stage model**

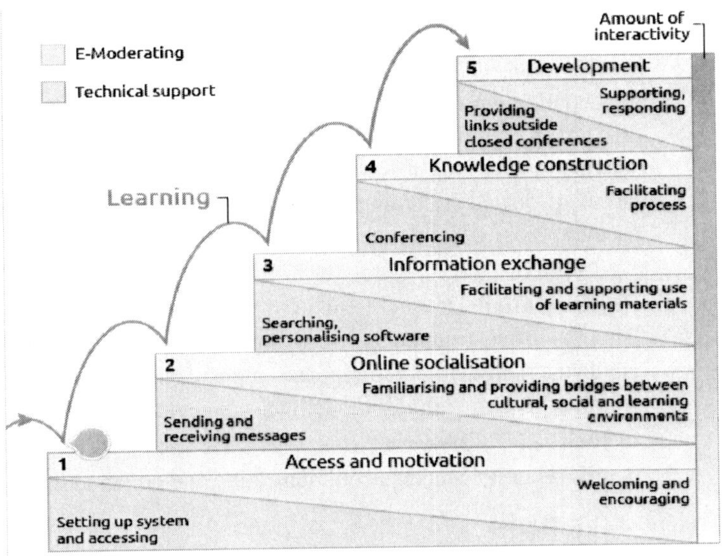


*Figure 1: Five Stage Model of Gilly Salmon*

## Major Elements of Gilly Salmon's five stage model

1. **E-tivities:** According to Dr Gilly Salmon, E-tivities are framework for enabling active and participative on-line learning by individuals and groups. It is important for online teaching and learning world. It helps to deploy useful principles and pedagogies for learning as well as network. E-tivities are utilized weekly and constantly through course module. It is to be deployed in the group of maximum 25 people. E-tivities according to Dr Gilly Salmon includes; Structured participative group work on online, Motivating, engaging, and purposeful in learning, Interaction between learners and active contribution, E-moderator (online teacher, tutor, trainer), Asynchronous mode of teaching, Simple text-based bulletin boards, On or offsite blended or online only.
2. **Scaffolding:** A structured learning scaffold offers essential support and development to participants at every stage. It means that teachers providing successive level of temporary support that helps students reach higher level of comprehension and skill acquisition.
3. **E-learning course:** According to Dr Salmon a typical course run over minimum five weeks. Each week allocated to develop a five-step learning process. The courses are in the form of distance learning. The participants from variety of geographical context 'meeting up' via computer messaging software.
4. **E-moderation:** It is a term used to describe a particular strategy of instruction between online instructor and their students. Moderator promotes human interaction and communication through modelling, conveying and building knowledge and skills.
5. **Conferencing:** Students communicating and collaborating.

## Merits of the Model

- Five stage model was constructed on the basis of experiences. It facilitates online networking and collaborative work.
- It was praised for its clarity. It was applied through structuring online project and programme

- Encouraging a trend towards on line pedagogy which is aligning with new technology.
- It highlighting the role of online tutor.
- There is an element of flexibility in teaching and learning

## LEARNERS AND NEW INFORMATION TECHNOLOGY

Technology plays an essential role to deliver education to the students outside of school. Commendably, all countries were able to deploy remote learning technologies using a combination of TV, Radio, Online, and Mobile Platforms. Technology has an increasingly significant impact, and such broad implications for every individual and group must use, apply Information and Technology in an effective, efficient, and ethical manner. Technology will serve today's students well, in entry-level work and beyond, in further study and lifelong learning, and their personal lives as inquisitive, reflective, discerning, and caring citizens. Advanced technologies are more pervasive today than they have ever been, and their uses are expanding continually.

Information technology has affected every aspect of human activity and possesses an important role to play in the field of education, especially in distance education to transform into an innovative experience. The need for new technologies in the teaching-learning process became stronger and faster. The new era of information becomes an age of knowledge, providing sound and unmatched feasibility for discovery, information exchange, communication, and exploration to strengthen the teaching and learning process. Information technology help in promoting opportunities for knowledge sharing throughout the world. For the updated information in educational institutions for teachers and students, this helps very much. Students are independent and they can make the best decisions possible about their studies, learning time, place, and resources. Students can work in collaborative and interactive learning environments effectively communicating, sharing information, and exchanging ideas and learning experiences with everything in the environment.

One of the basic functions of education is to prepare students for the well-being of their life. In the 21$^{st}$ century, education is provided for all. In India, basic education is given equally without any social and cultural discrimination. For better learning, sharing information is an essential thing. Information encompasses and relies on the use of different channels of communication, which can be presently called Information and Communication Technology.

Technology has changed the scenario of education particularly, pedagogy and instruction making the teaching-learning process more productive creating collaborative, learner-centred, and interactive global learning environments. Information technologies are assumed to play a constructive role in education to make the teaching and learning process more productive through collaboration in an information-rich society. The Information-rich society promotes new practices and paradigms for education where the teacher has to play a new role of mentoring, coaching, and helping students in their studies rather than to play the conventional role of spoon-feeding in the classroom. Students can learn independently having a wide choice of program selection and access to information students can interact and share learning experiences with their teaching and fellow learners in the knowledge construction and dissemination process.

The history of Information storage and dissemination indicates that human beings use different things for information storage, its display, and transmission. At different ages, people used different materials and methods for communication such as rocks and stones, papyrus, palm leaves, animal leather, and handicraft manuscripts for storing and transmitting. Information from one place to another. At present, knowledge may be regarded as power and it comes from information. Information encompasses and relies upon the use of different communication channels or technologies are called information technology.

## New trends in Education Technology in IT 2020-2021

In this current trending scenario, Education Technology had been drastically changed. The Covid-19 Pandemic has moved the classroom situation into networking online classes. Technology is an innovation of humans, so when an educator applies technology in teaching, it is also innovative. It allows teachers to provide multimedia to address diverse learning styles such as animation, live classes, etc. The technology used in education in current trends are,

## E-learning

E-learning comprises all forms of electronically supported learning and teaching. The information and communication systems, whether networked or not, serve as specific media to implement the learning process. It is an instructional content or learning experience delivered or enabled by electronic technologies. It allows you to learn anywhere and usually at any time, as long as you have a properly configured computer. It can be CD-ROM-based network-based, Internet-based, or Intranet based. The features of e-learning as under:

- E-Learning is dynamic
- E-Learning operates in Real-time
- It is collaborative
- It is individualistic
- It is comprehensive
- It has a synchronous and asynchronous communication style

## Video-assisted learning

Video-assisted learning (VAL) is defined as a strategic teaching approach to using videos – either educational or conceptual – to improve a student's comprehension, cognitive ability, or social-emotional skills. It includes virtual reality, virtual classroom, virtual laboratory, etc.

**Virtual Reality (VR):** A term that applies to computer-simulated environments that allows a participant to believe and barely distinguish a virtual experience from a real one.

**Virtual Classroom (VC):** A simulated classroom via the internet that provides a convenient communication environment for distance learners just like a traditional face-to-face classroom.

**Virtual Laboratory (VL):** An environment in which experiments are conducted or controlled partly or wholly through computer operation, simulation, animation either locally or remotely via the internet.

## Block-chain Technology

Blockchain technology is a structure that stores transactional records, also known as the block, of the public in several databases, known as the "chain," in a network connected through peer-to-peer nodes. Typically, this storage is referred to as a 'digital ledger.' the digital ledger is like a Google spreadsheet shared among numerous computers in a network, in which, the transactional records are stored based on actual purchases. The fascinating angle is that anybody can see the data, but they can't corrupt it.

## Big Data

Big Data and analytics technologies enable your organization to become more competitive and grow without limits. data scientists break big data into four dimensions: volume, variety, velocity, and veracity. For many people, this term is directly associated with "a lot of data". Understanding this technology in this way, however, is not entirely accurate. Big Data technology implies: Compilation, Storage, and Exploitation.

## Artificial Intelligence

It is a simulation of human intelligence processes by machines, especially computer systems. These processes include learning, reasoning, and self-correction. Specific applications of AI include expert systems, natural language processing, speech recognition, and machine vision. There are four types of artificial intelligence: reactive machines, limited memory, theory of mind, and self-awareness. The basic goal of AI is to enable computers and machines to perform intellectual tasks such as problem-solving, decision making, perception, and understanding human communication.

## Learning analytics

Learning analytics is the measurement, collection, analysis, and reporting of data about learners and their contexts, for purposes of understanding and optimizing learning and the environments in which it occurs, as defined back in 2011 for the first LAK, this general definition still holds even as the field has grown. Learning analytics is both an academic field and commercial marketplace which have taken rapid shape over the last decade. As a research and teaching field, Learning Analytics sits at the convergence of Learning (e.g. educational research, learning and assessment sciences, educational technology), Analytics (e.g. statistics, visualization, computer/data sciences, artificial intelligence), and Human-Centred Design (e.g. usability, participatory design, sociotechnical systems thinking). Learning analytics has the potential to transform the way we measure impact and outcomes in learning environments - enabling providers to develop new ways of achieving excellence in teaching and learning, providing students with new information to make the best choice about their education.

## Gamification

Gamification is adding game mechanics into nongame environments, like a website, online community, learning management system, or business' intranet to increase participation. The goal of gamification is to engage with consumers, employees, and partners to inspire collaboration, share and interact. A gamification strategy is a process of taking something that already exists – like a software application or online community – and using gaming techniques to motivate consistent participation and long-term engagement.

## Immersive learning with VR and AR

This is where virtual reality (VR) and augmented reality (AR) can add real value to the learning process. These "extended reality" (XR) technologies can create immersive worlds where students can visualize concepts and interactively learn new skills and information. Combining traditional teaching methods with cutting-edge AR/VR-based learning solutions makes learning uniquely immersive for students, now more digitally aware and tech-savvy than ever before. AR/VR technology allows for multisensory (or multimodal) learning and brings together visual, auditory, kinaesthetic, and tactile elements for a fully immersive experience.

## STEAM

STEAM is an educational approach to learning that uses Science, Technology, Engineering, the Arts, and Mathematics as access points for guiding student inquiry, dialogue, and critical thinking. STEAM stands for Science, Technology, Engineering, Art, and Math. Each of STEAM's five subjects shares a common approach and focus. Steam offers digital rights management (DRM), server hosting, video streaming, and social networking services. It also provides the user with installation and automatic updating of games, and community features such as friends lists and groups, cloud storage, and in-game voice and chats functionality.

## Social media in learning

Social media in education refers to the practice of using social media platforms as a way to enhance the education of students. Social media is defined as "a group of Internet-based applications that build on the ideological and technological foundations and that allow the creation and exchange of user-generated content. Social media promotes self-directed learning, which prepares students to search for answers and make decisions independently. When reinforced in a classroom setting, these social media skills can be guided and refined to produce better learning outcomes and critical awareness.

## Significance of IT in Education

- **Access to a variety of learning resources:** In the era of technology, IT aids plenty of resources to enhance teaching skills and learning ability. With the help of IT now it is easy to provide audio-visual education. The learning resources are being widened and widened. Now with this vivid and vast technique as part of the IT curriculum, learners are encouraged to regard computers as tools to be used in all aspects of their studies. In particular, they need to make use of the new multimedia technologies to communicate ideas, describe projects, and order information in their work.
- **Immediacy to information:** IT has provided immediacy to education. Now in the year of computers and web networks, the pace of imparting knowledge is very fast and one can be educated anywhere at any time. New IT has often been introduced into well-established patterns of working and living without radically altering them. For example, the traditional office, with secretaries working at keyboards and notes being written on paper and manually exchanged, has remained remarkably stable, even if personal computers have replaced typewriters.
- **Any time learning:** Now in the year of computers and web networks, the pace of imparting knowledge is very fast

and one can be educated. One can study whenever he wills irrespective of whether it is day or night and irrespective of being in India or the US because of the boom in IT.

- **Collaborative learning:** Now IT has made it easy to study as well as teach in groups or clusters. Online we can be united together to do the desired task. Efficient postal systems, the telephone (fixed and mobile), and various recording and playback systems based on computer technology all have a part to play in educational broadcasting in the new millennium. The Internet and its Web sites are now familiar to many children in developed countries and among educational elites elsewhere, but it remains of little significance to very many more, who lack the most basic means for subsistence.
- **Multimedia approach to education:** Audio-Visual Education, planning, preparation, and use of devices and materials that involve sight, sound, or both, for educational purposes. Among the devices used are still and motion pictures, filmstrips, television, transparencies, audiotapes, records, teaching machines, computers, and videodiscs. The growth of audio-visual education has reflected developments in both technology and learning theory. Studies in the psychology of learning suggest that the use of audio-visuals in education has several advantages. All learning is based on perception, the process by which the senses gain information from the environment. The higher processes of memory and concept formation cannot occur without prior perception. People can attend to only a limited amount of information at a time; their selection and perception of information are influenced by past experiences. Researchers have found that other conditions being equal, more information is taken in if it is received simultaneously in two modalities (vision and hearing, for example) rather than in a single modality. Furthermore, learning is enhanced when the material is organized and that organization is evident to the student. These findings suggest the value of audio-visuals in the educational process. They can facilitate perception of the most important features, can be carefully organized, and can require the student to use more than one modality.

- **Authentic and up to date information:** The information and data which are available on the net are purely correct and up to date. Internet, a collection of computer networks that operate to common standards and enable the computers and the programs they run to communicate directly provides true and correct information.
- **Online library:** Internets support thousands of different kinds of operational and experimental services one of which is an online library. We can get plenty of data from this online library. As part of the IT curriculum, learners are encouraged to regard computers as tools to be used in all aspects of their studies. In particular, they need to make use of the new multimedia technologies to communicate ideas, describe projects, and order information in their work. This requires them to select the medium best suited to conveying their message, structure information hierarchically, and link together information to produce a multidimensional document.
- **Distance learning:** Distance Learning, method of learning at a distance rather than in a classroom. Late 20th-century communications technologies, in their most recent phases multimedia and interactive, open up new possibilities, both individual and institutional, for an unprecedented expansion of home-based learning, much of it part-time. The term distance learning was coined within the context of a continuing communications revolution, largely replacing a hitherto confusing mixed nomenclature home study, independent study, external study, and, most common, though restricted in pedagogic means, correspondence study. The convergence of increased demand for access to educational facilities and innovative communications technology has been increasingly exploited in face of criticisms that distance learning is an inadequate substitute for learning alongside other informal institutions. A powerful incentive has been reduced costs per student. At the same time, students studying at home themselves save on travel time and other costs. Whatever the reasoning, distance learning widens access for students unable for whatever reason (course availability, geographical remoteness, family circumstances, individual

disability) to study alongside others. At the same time, it appeals to students who prefer learning at home. In addition, it appeals to organizers of professional and business education, providing an incentive to rethink the most effective way of communicating vital information.

- **Better access to children with disabilities:** Information technology has brought drastic changes in the life of disabled children. IT provides various software and technique to educate these poor people. Unless provided early with special training, people profoundly deaf from birth are incapable of learning to speak. Deafness from birth causes severe sensory deprivation, which can seriously affect a person's intellectual capacity or ability to learn. A child who sustains a hearing loss early in life may lack the language stimulation experienced by children who can hear. The critical period for neurological plasticity is up to age seven.

In short, the integration of information technology in teaching is a central matter in ensuring quality in the educational system. There are two equally important reasons for integrating information technology in teaching. Pupils must become familiar with the use of information technology, since all jobs in the society of the future will be dependent on it, and information technology must be used in teaching to improve its quality and make it more effective.

## CONCLUSION

In conclusion, Unit 2 has provided a comprehensive overview of modern instructional approaches that are reshaping education in the digital age. We have explored a variety of concepts and methodologies, from technology-enhanced learning (TEL) and cloud computing to mobile learning (M-learning) and ubiquitous learning (U-learning). Through the lens of instructional design, we have delved into the significance of concept mapping, mind mapping, and the application of models of teaching in curriculum development. Moreover, we have examined the foundational frameworks such as Bloom's Taxonomy and standardized achievement tests, which continue to guide educators in designing effective learning experiences. Additionally, we have explored contemporary models like Laurillard's conversational model and the five-stage model of Gilly Salmon, which emphasize interactive and participatory learning environments. As education continues to evolve, it is essential for educators to embrace these modern instructional approaches to meet the diverse needs of learners and foster meaningful engagement in the learning process. By leveraging technology, adapting curriculum development strategies, and incorporating innovative pedagogical models, educators can create dynamic learning experiences that empower students to thrive in an ever-changing world. Thus, this chapter underscores the importance of continuous learning and adaptation to ensure the effectiveness and relevance of educational practices in the digital era.

## REFERENCES

1. Alexander, B. (2004). *Going Nomadic: Mobile Learning in Higher Education*. Educause
2. Alkhawaldeh, A. (2020). Reflections by some Jordanian EFL lecturers on Salmon's five-stage e-learning model and its possible application to teaching English in Jordan. *International Journal of English Linguistics*, *10*(2), 229-243.
3. Andrews, D. and L. Goodson. (1980). A Comparative Analysis of Models of Instructional Design. *Journal of Instructional Development, 3*(4), 2-16.
4. Attewell, J., & Savill-Smith, C. (2005). *Mobile Learning Anytime Everywhere*. Learning and Skills Development Agency.
5. Ausubel, D. P. (1960). The use of advance organizers in the learning and retention of meaningful verbal material. *Journal of Educational Psychology*.
6. Ausubel, David P. (1963). *The Psychology of Meaningful Verbal Learning*. New York:
7. Ausubel, David P. (1967). *Learning Theory and classroom Practice*. Ontario: The Ontario Institute for Studies in Education.
8. Ausubel, David P. (1968). *Educational Psychology, A Cognitive View*. New York: Holt, Rinehart and Winston, Inc.
9. Baran, E. (2014). A Review of Research on Mobile Learning in Teacher Education. *Educational Technology & Society, 17*(4),17-32. https://www.jstor.org/stable/jeductechsoci.17.4.17
10. Braden, R.A. (1996). The Case for Linear Instructional Design and Development: A Commentary on Models, Challenges and Myths. *Educational Technology.*
11. Briggs, L.J., K.L. Gustafson, and M.H. Tillman. (1991). *Instructional Design: Principles and Applications*. 2nd ed. New Jersey: Educational Technology Publications, Inc.
12. Bruce, R. Joyce and Marsha, Weil (2008). *Models of Teaching* (8th Edition), Allyn & Bacon.

13. Bruce, R. Joyce, Marsha Weil and Emily, Calhoun (2005). *Models of Teaching* (7th Edition): My Lab School Edition.
14. Clinch, P. (2005), *Supporting law teaching: training and teaching*, Presentation at UKCLE seminar on teaching and learning for legal skills trainers, 16 February 2005,
15. Derrida, J. (2006). *Writing and Diff*erence (A. Bass, Trans.). Routledge.
16. Dick, W. & W. Carey. (1990). *Systematic Design of Instruction*. 3rd ed. Glenview, IL: Harper Collins.
17. Dijkstra, S., N. Seel, F. Schott, and R.D. (1997). *Instructional Design; International Perspectives*, New Jersey: Lawrence Erlbaum Associates.
18. Fullan, M. (2007). *The New Meaning of Educational Change*. (7th Ed.). Teachers College
19. Gagné, R.M. & M.P. Driscoll. (1988). *Essentials of Learning for Instruction*. 2nd ed. New Jersey: Prentice-Hall.
20. Gagné, R.M., & W. Dick. (1983). "Instructional Psychology." *Annual Review of Psychology, 34* 261-295.
21. Gropper, G.L. "On Gaining Acceptance for Instructional Design in A University Setting." Education/Technology, 17 (1977), 7-12.
22. Johnson, K.A. & L.J. Foa. (1989). *Instructional Design: Alternatives for Effective Education and Training*. New York: American Council on Education and Macmillan Publishing Company.
23. Jonassen, D.H., Beissneer K., and Yacci, M.A. (1993) *Structural Knowledge: Techniques for Conveying, Assessing, and Acquiring Structural Knowledge*. Hillsdale, NJ: Lawrence Erlbaum Associates.
24. Jovanović, J., Gašević, D., Knight, C., & Richards, G. (2007). Ontologies for Effective Use of Context in e-Learning Settings. *Educational Technology & Society, 10* (3), 47-59.
25. Kemp, J.E. and D.C. Smellie. (1989). *Planning, Producing and Using Instructional Media*. New York: Harper & Row.
26. King, J. P. (2006). *One Hundred Philosophers: A Guide to World's Greatest Thinkers* (2nd Ed.), Aplle Press.
27. Kinshuk, G.S. (2012) Ubiquitous Learning. In: Seel N.M. (eds) *Encyclopaedia of the Sciences of Learning*. Springer, Boston, MA. https://doi.org/10.1007/978-1-4419-1428-6_224
28. Laurillard, D. (2007). *Pedagogical forms for mobile learning: framing research questions*, London Knowledge Lab Institute of Education, London https://discovery.ucl.ac.uk/id/eprint/10000627/1/Mobile_C6_Laurillard.pdf
29. Laurillard, D. (2012). *Teaching as a Design Science: Building Pedagogical Patterns for Learning and Technology*, Taylor & Francis Group, London. Available from: ProQuest Ebook Central. [20 February 2022].

30. Laurillard, D. (2008). The teacher as action researcher: Using technology to capture pedagogic form. *Studies in Higher Education, 33*(2), 139-154.
31. Laurillard, D. (2009). The Pedagogical Challenges to Collaborative Technologies. *International Journal of Computer-Supported Collaborative Learning. 4,* 5-20. 10.1007/s11412-008-9056-2.
32. Leshin, C.B., J. Pollock, and M. Reigeluth. (1992). *Instructional Design Strategies and Tactics*. New Jersey: Educational Technology Publications.
33. Lockwood, F. (1992). *Activities in Self-Instructional Texts*. London: Kogan Page.
34. Lockwood, F., ed. (1994). *Materials Production in Open and Distance Learning*. London: Paul Chapman Publishing.
35. Lowe, R. (1993). *Successful Instructional Diagrams*. London: Kogan Page.
36. Lösel, F., & Beelmann, A. (2003). Effects of child skills training in preventing antisocial behavior: A systematic review of randomized evaluations. *Annals of the American Academy of Political and Social Science*, 587, 84-109.
37. McBeath, R.J. (1992). *Instructing and Evaluating in Higher Education: A Guidebook for Planning Learning Outcomes*. New Jersey: Educational Technology Publications.
38. Mize, J., & Cox, R. A. (1990). Social knowledge and social competence: Number and quality of strategies as predictors of peer behaviour. *Journal of Genetic Psychology*, 151,117-127.
39. Moore, N.A.J. (2002). Review of E-moderating—the key to teaching and learning online. *Language Learning & Technology*, *6*(3), 21-24.
40. Oberoi, S.C., (2004) *Educational Technology*, New Delhi, Arya Book Depot.
41. Nadler, L. & Z. Nadler. (1994). *Designing Training Programs - The Critical Events Model*. Houston: Gulf Publishing Company.
42. Novak, J.D. (1991) "Clarify with Concept Maps: A tool for students and teachers alike," *The Science Teacher, 58*(7), 45-49.
43. Hirtz, S., & Harper, D.M. (Eds.), *Education for a Digital World: Advice, Guidelines, and Effective Practice from Around the Globe* (pp. 51-56), Commonwealth of Learning.
44. Seels, B. & Z. Glasgow. (1990). *Exercises in Instructional Design*. New Jersey: Charles Merrill.
45. Reigeluth, C. M., ed. (1983). *Instructional Design Theories and Models*. New Jersey: Erlbaum.
46. Rowntree, D. (1990). *Teaching Through Self-Instruction: How to Develop Open Learning Materials*. London: Kogan Page.
47. Sharma, R.A., (2013) *Educational Technology and Management*, R. Lal Book Depot.
48. Smith, P.L. & Ragan, T.J. (1999). *Instructional Design*. New York: Macmillan Publishing Company,

49. Tahir, Zurainee & Haron, Haryani & Kaur, Jasber. (2018). Ubiquitous Learning Environment and Technologies: A Review. *International Journal of Engineering and Technology,* 7(1), 31-35. 10.14419/ijet.v7i3.15.17402.

50. Ting, Y. R. (2005). Mobile Learning: Current Trend and future Challenges. *Proceedings of the Fifth International Conference on Advanced Learning Technologies*, Los Alamitos, IEEE Computer Society Press.

51. Uden, L. (2007). Activity Theory for Designing Mobile Learning. *Journal of Mobile Learning and Organisation, 1*(1), 81-102.

52. Wilson, S. J., Lipsey, M. W., & Derzon, J. H. (2003). The effects of school violence prevention programs on aggressive and disruptive behaviour. *Journal of Consulting and Clinical Psychology, 7*(1), 136-149.

53. Yahya, S., Ahmad, E. & Abd Jalil, K. (2010). The definition and characteristics of ubiquitous learning: A discussion. *International Journal of Education and Development using ICT, 6*(1), Open Campus, The University of the West Indies, West Indies. Retrieved March 28, 2022 from https://www.learntechlib.org/p/188069/.

# Unit - 3

# Quality Improvement in Primary Education

## INTRODUCTION

Since independence, India has made considerable progress in the field of primary education. At elementary level the achievement of the target of free and compulsory education as directed by the Constitution is a great challenge. It is seen that the objectives of universalization of elementary education are being achieved gradually. But the rate of achievement in respect of different aspects like the condition necessary for providing access to elementary education, increasing enrolment of students in primary and upper primary schools, enhancing the retention of students and also the levels of their achievement in different classes are gradually improving. Primary education is the largest sub-sector of any education system. Too many children in the world today grow up without this chance. Education should be able to bring out the best qualities in a person. The role of education in facilitating social and economic progress is well recognized. Primary education covering reading, writing and arithmetic is considered as a crucial aspect of quality of life.

Every human being should have the opportunity to make a better life for themselves. Unfortunately, too many children in the world today grow up without this chance, because they are denied their basic right to even attend primary school. A sustainable end to world poverty as we know it, as well as the path to peace and security, requires that citizens in every country are empowered to make positive choices and provide for themselves and their families. Today's education system does not deliver quality education. Education should be able to bring out the best qualities in a person above all the right to discern and a sense of curiosity which would mould him into an empowered individual to take on the complexities of life, Wipro Chairman Azim Premji said.

The World Education Forum (2000) agreed on Educations for All (EFA) goals. The sixth goal concerned Education Quality, '.... improving all aspects of the quality of education and ensuring excellence of all so that recognized and measurable learning outcomes are achieved by all, especially in literacy, numeracy and essential life skills. Presently it has been stipulated that the objectives of elementary education are to be attained by the year 2025. Much efforts had been made for the qualitative improvement of primary education in our country. Attempts have been made both by the state and centre by establishing various agencies for quality improvement of elementary education. These organisations play a pivotal role in the whole scheme of raising the quality of primary education in the country. The roles of various organisation for the qualitative improvement of primary education are listed below.

## DISTRICT INSTITUTE OF EDUCATION AND TRAINING (DIET)

DIET have been opened by the Government as per the Programme of Action (POA-86 and 92 in order to provide better training to future teachers. The National Policy on Education 1986 and programme of action envisaged an important innovation in the shape of District Institutes of Education and Training (DIET) for providing quantitatively wider coverage as well as qualitatively better support and facilities. Mainly there are three functions of a DIET:

- **Training and Orientation**: Functions relating to Training and Orientation are as follows: (a) Pre-service and in-service education of teacher for the formal school system, (b) Induction level and continuing education of non-formal and adult education instructors and supervisors, (c) Orientation of community leaders, functionaries of voluntary organisations, (d) Training and orientation of heads of institutions in institutional planning and management and micro-level planning.

- **Resources Support includes the following**: (a) Academic support to school complex and District Boards of education. (b) Serving as evaluation centre for primary and upper primary schools as well as non-formal and adult education programmes. (c) Provision of services of resources and learning centres for teachers and instructors.
- **Action Research includes the following**: (a) Conducting experiments to deal with specific problem of the district in achieving the objectives in the areas of elementary and adult education. (b) Creating motivation among the teachers to undertake educational innovations and action research project.

## 'QUALITY' IN EDUCATION

The quality of education is concerned with a child's experience of education-an-amalgamation of the school, teachers, teaching as well as the nature of infrastructure and facilities. 'Quality' as a term refers to 'how well' certain objects and processes achieve their given aims. Quality in education requires an appreciation of the aims of education; the social and philosophical roots of these aims as well as determining the nature of the organization and system that is best oriented to achieve them. Educational quality concerns typically encompass topics such as teacher-training, textbooks and materials, evaluation and physical infrastructure especially school buildings. The purpose of universalizing elementary education is to bring to every child at a bare minimum, the ability to participate in social, political and economic processes. To define quality in the field of education, it may be instructive to examine the more widely practiced usage of quality and explore its appropriateness or applicability for education. Quality is contextual not comprehensive. The quest for quality has been the major concern of the entire human civilization. Quality is not an act; it is a habit. It generally signifies the degree of excellence.

### Concept of Quality in Primary Education

Quality is therefore directly related to what occurs in two educational contexts; Firstly, in the more focused environment of the classroom; Secondly in the wider context of the school system and social context in which the classroom is embedded. Both environments have a reciprocal relationship with each other. Quality, means relevance to context, to needs (both 'needs now' and 'needs later') and to humanity. Efficiency in setting standards, in meeting standards set and in improving standards; Expectations beyond the normal education system of a school. Which means, A relevant, efficient and special education must, in other words, be available to all children irrespective of gender, ability or wealth.

## Drawbacks of Primary Education

To iron out the immediate problems faced in the implementation of primary education goals, some drawbacks of primary education are:

- Inadequate / absence of access to a comparable quality of education
- Overcrowding in the existing government schools
- Mismatches between the demand and supply of schooling facilities
- Dilapidated condition of classrooms, particularly those running in rented buildings
- Unsatisfactory teaching-learning process
- Lack of sanitation and water facilities in old school buildings
- Excessive reliance on centrally sponsored schemes has also created its own problems. The states seldom initiate programmes of educational development at their own initiatives and wait for central government initiatives

## Techniques for Improving the Quality of Primary Education

## Operation Black-Board

According to the National Policy on Education 1986, a scheme of Operation Blackboard was launched in 1987. The main objective of this scheme was to provide minimum essential facilities to all primary schools in the country. Operation Black board is a centrally sponsored scheme which has been implemented in different states to bring qualitative improvements it's in elementary education. The NPE recommended the launching of a phased drive, symbolically called operation Blackboard, as centrally sponsored scheme. It is aimed at bringing about substantial improvement in the facilities of primary schools run by Government, Local Bodies and Panchayat Raj and recognized aided institutions. The components of operation black board are:

- Provision of a building comprising at least two reasonable large all-weather rooms with a deep veranda and separate toilet facilities for boys and girls.
- At least two teachers in every school, as far as possible, one of them a woman and
- Provision of essential teaching and learning materials including black boards, maps, charts, toys and equipment for work experience.

Operation Blackboard is one of the priority strategies for Universalisation of Elementary Education. NPE and its programme of Action recommended that 100% central assistance is to be provided for the appointment of the second teacher in the single teacher schools and for purchase of materials.

- **Quality Infrastructure:** The most important equity issue considering that almost 85% of the children in our country are in government school and they deserve much better school.
- **The Attitude of the Teacher:** The most important aspect of the approach is the attitude of the teacher, which should be that learning is a form of play which fosters the blossoming of the child's nature development. Learning should and can be made interesting, enjoyable and fun.
- **Teaching Materials:** A large portion of the teaching materials are produced at the school by the teachers, who customize their teaching aids suit the interests and knowledge levels of students.
- **Evaluating the Status of Learning:** The current status of the learning assessment was quite revealing. Surprisingly, 50% of the children in any village could not read fluently and 70% of the children attending school didn't understand the basic concepts of numbers and arithmetic. To tackle these underachievement patterns, simplifying the evaluation becomes a natural choice.
- **Teacher - Pupil Ratio:** Several surveys, researches and reports have established the current poor quality beyond doubt it is only because of the teacher-pupil ratio. The current

national average is 1:40. Elementary Education Budgets has suggested that the quality is probably the best when the ratio is between 1:25 to 1:35.

- **Demonstrating the Change:** To demonstrate a change requires multi-pronged and strategic reforms in teaching. Focus on specific goals or skills, assessing what the children know, designing activities specific to the child's level, recognizing small improvements and using all these to change perceptions of children's activities, were discussed as change factors.
- **Mid-Day Meal Quality:** The decision to provide mid-day meal to all children in elementary schools was the best thing to happen and has positively impacted health, attendance and reduction in drop-out rates.

## Equitable and Inclusive Education

NEP 2020 aims to ensure that no child loses any opportunity to learn and excel because of the circumstances of birth or background. Special emphasis will be given on Socially and Economically Disadvantaged Groups (SEDGs) which include gender, socio-cultural, and geographical identities and disabilities.

## The Act of Teaching

The act of teaching consists primarily of presenting sensory images, objects and information to the child in a pleasant and interesting manner and permitting the child to observe and inquire about the subject, without compelling the child to memorize. Coloured flash cards with large images are utilized as convenient, low-cost teaching aids.

## Curriculum Reviewed and Reformed

There is a clear need for relevant curricula in order to provide quality education. Curricula must be regularly reviewed and reformed to reflect these changes and to adequately prepare pupils to respond to their environment and its challenges. UNESCO is implementing a number of activities worldwide that include curriculum strategy, curriculum development and reform, textbook revision, training and publications. UNESCO International Bureau of Education (IBE) has a mandate to support and strengthen national capacity to lead and facilitate renewal of curricula and to adopt the context and methods of school education. They are focused on a host of curriculum development issues ranging from management of curriculum reform, to citizenship education, multiculturalism, social exclusion, non-violence and learning to live together through the teaching of history and geography.

## New Approaches to Active Pedagogical Learning

New approaches to active pedagogical learning and innovative modalities need to be developed to encourage teachers to change from using a traditional lecture approach to a more interactive style of teaching. Pedagogical techniques should include participatory and gender-sensitive teaching and learning methods and strategies that foster critical thinking and problem-solving skills. Rapid Acquisition of Basic

- **Math Skills:** Rapid acquisition of basic math skills is achieved through the use of number line method which enables the child to physically experiment and act out differently combinations of addition and subtraction.
- **Storytelling:** Story telling is used to make learning fun and to communicate basic values of goodness, beauty, harmony, responsibility and right conduct. Information on people and living things, places, history, geography and other cultures are presented to the child in the form of stories, pictorial information and explanations combined together to present facts in a living, integrated context rather than as a series of separate divorced subjects.
- **Evaluation Methodologies:** As an answer to the various problems posed by current scenario (such as meaningless aggregation of skills etc.), evaluation methodologies can be evolved in the direction of skill-by-skill testing, competing with oneself rather than others, and providing adequate opportunities to better one's performance.

In short, the concern for quality of education has been voiced from time to time in India. The National Policy on Education (NPE), 1986 and the revised NPE, 1992 and NEP 2020 highlighted the urgency to address the quality concerns on priority basis. Quality can't improve by itself. It requires multi-pronged and strategic reforms in teacher-training; improvements in the facilities and infrastructure in schools; teacher's motivation; and a change in the style of teaching to make it attractive to the students. The policy also recommended that a system of continuous and comprehensive evaluation would be established. Besides the state level schemes to improve access and quality of education, a number of centrally sponsored schemes and externally funded projects, undertaken in the recent years, are experimenting with various models of bringing about increased coverage, retention and improvements in quality.

## RECOMMENDATIONS OF EDUCATIONAL COMMISSIONS

India gained independence on 15th August 1947. Since independence, the government of India has set up various commissions and education committees in the field of education, intending to build a new higher education infrastructure throughout India. The result is unimaginable change and development in the field of education in India. The main objectives of these commissions and committees are to address the challenges of education, recommend comprehensive education policies, and improve the education system in India. Several commissions and committees address education development at different stages in this country. Some of them which had a bearing on elementary education are the following:

- Radhakrishnan Commission (1948-49)
- Mudaliyar Commission (1952)
- National Committee on Women's Education (1958)
- Kothari Commission (1964-66)
- Yashpal Committee (1992)
- National Education Policy (1968)
- National Education Policy (1986)
- Ramamurti Review Committee (1990)
- Janardhana Reddy Committee (1992)

On the eve of independence, the educational situation was dire. Despite all that had been accomplished under British rule, we started our freedom with a relatively low level of educational attainment in almost all areas. There were 17 of them. There are 5,297 universities and 636 colleges (with a total enrolment of 2,38,000 students), universities, and 636 colleges (with a total enrolment of 2,38,000 students). Secondary schools with 8,70,000 students (implying that not a single adolescent was present). In the age group 14-17, one out of every twenty was enrolled in school). There were 12,843 middle schools with two million students (only one out of every eleven children in the age group 11-14 were enrolled) and 1,72,661 primary schools with fourteen million students. (This meant that only one child in every three in the age group 6-years-old was a pupil.) 11 was a student). Technical and vocational education were underdeveloped at the school and university levels and the supply of highly qualified individuals. Scientific talent was scarce. There were significant educational disparities. Particularly between regions, between urban and rural areas. On the one hand, there are differences between men and women and between advanced and intermediate castes. The educational standards were generally unsatisfactory, especially at the school level, with too much focus on English and too little on Mathematics, Science, or Indian culture.

## UNIVERSITY EDUCATION COMMISSION (1948-49)

The University Education Commission (1948-49) was the first post-independence commission on education. It focused primarily on higher education, but it also addressed concerns related to school education. The Commission was tasked with **Dr S Radhakrishnan**, a great visionary who was named as chairman. This is a new age. The Radhakrishnan Commission on University Education described higher education's critical functions. The goals of universities should be to develop capable people who can effectively carry out national obligations in a variety of fields. The university is an educational institution that has to produce skilled managers and staff in a variety of areas as well as industries. It must provide excellent leadership in various fields nation's best interests. The Commission proposed that the requirement for admission to university courses be the same as the current intermediate test, that is, after 12 years of schooling and middle college. It remarked that "our secondary education remains the weakest link in our educational machinery and needs urgent reforms." The Commission stated that school education aims to provide good general education. It defined the elements of a good education as "not only preparing students for university work but also preparing them for life." If he did not go to university, he would have to work to support himself. According to the Commission, the roles of a school and a university should be distinct. The aim of a school should be to provide appropriate education to those who intend to pursue higher education and those who do not, of going any further. The teaching of both groups could be merged, whereas some schools may be able to prepare students for careers in agriculture and commerce. The University Education Commission emphasized integrating general education into the school curriculum. The Commission was adamant that the school's results be diverse enough that many people could easily participate. A few people will continue working or self-employed in real-life-research outside of the classroom.

## SECONDARY EDUCATION COMMISSION (1952-53)

The National Commissions – the Secondary Education Commission (1952-53) and the Education Commission (1964-66) – revisited the questions about education expressed during the freedom struggle (1964-66). Both commissions produced detailed reports on the themes that emerged from Mahatma Gandhi's educational ideology in the twentieth century, a shift in the socio-political landscape emphasizing national developments (NCF, Source: 2005, p.3). Under the terms of the law, a separate education commission was created. In 1952, under **Dr Lakshamanaswami Mudaliyar,** the issues were linked to school education. According to the Commission Report of 1952, Schools must play a critical role in the development of democratic citizenship, with a focus on "Democracy is founded on confidence in the dignity and value of every "individual," whose inherent worth cannot be diminished by economic, ethnic, or social considerations (SEC, 1952, p.20)." In 1953, the Secondary Education Commission issued a report with recommendations on nearly every aspect of secondary education. The Commission's main findings were as follows:

- installation of higher secondary system;
- diversified courses;
- three language formula;
- emphasis on education and vocational guidance;

- improvement in building and equipment.
- improvement in methods of teaching, textbooks, and system of examination;

The Commission adopted the strategy of establishing a three-year national secondary education system (after eight years of elementary education). The proposal to break the intermediate stage into two sections, with one year spent in school and the other at university, proved to be backward – the eleven-year higher secondary course introduced specialization too early (after class VIII) and found it challenging to find work (Naik, 1969).

## Objectives of Mudaliyar Commission

- To study contemporary secondary education's condition and suggest measures for its reorganization.
- To study aims, curriculum & teaching standard of secondary education of every province in India.
- To check pay-scales & service conditions of secondary school teachers.
- To analyse the state of secondary schools in every region.
- To learn examination system of secondary level.
- To study problems of secondary education in every region & suggest their remedies.

## Report of Mudaliyar Commission

Commission adopted two methods to study existing secondary education in every region of India. (a) Questionnaire Method, (b) Interview Method. Based on information acquired through these two methods, the commission prepared its report and presented it to Govt of India on 29th August 1953. This report is 244 pages divided into 14 chapters. The report consists of; (a) Shortcomings of the then existing system of secondary education, (b) Remedies and detailed features of secondary education.

**Defects of the Existing System**: The main aim of secondary education is to prepare students to get admission in university education, but it does not develop qualities such as cooperation, discipline and leadership among students.

- The curriculum of secondary education is impractical.
- Teaching methods are full of defects.
- The examination system is full of flaws.
- Rigid time-table and unsuitable textbooks.
- No proper arrangements of co-curricular activities in the schools.
- No proper criteria for the appointment of teachers.

**Suggestions regarding Secondary Education**

- It should be for children in the age group 11-17 years.
- Its duration should be seven years.
- It should be divided into two parts: Junior secondary stage (3 years) and Higher secondary stage (4 years).
- Intermediate classes should be abolished, and class 11th should be added to secondary education and class 12th to degree courses.
- Multipurpose schools should be opened at the higher secondary level, and diversified methods should be introduced.
- Special schools for disabled children.

**Suggestions regarding Aims of Secondary Education**

- Development of democratic citizenship
- Development of vocational skills
- Development of personality
- Development of leadership qualities

**Suggestions regarding curriculum at secondary level**

- Related to real life
- Extensive and flexible
- Subjects and activities should be inter-related
- Enable students to utilize their leisure

**Suggestions regarding Educational and Vocational Guidance and Counselling**

- Educational and vocational guidance Bureau should be established in every province.

- Guidance and counselling services should be organized in every secondary school. To conduct this service, career masters and guidance officers should be appointed.
- The central government should manage the training of career masters and guidance officers.
- Guidance should be provided based on their differences, interests, attitude, aptitude & ability.

## Curriculum for Junior Secondary Education

- Mother's tongue
- The national language is Hindi (whose mother tongue is not Hindi) or another federal language (whose mother tongue is Hindi).
- English
- Social science
- General science
- Mathematics
- Arts and music
- Handicrafts
- Physical education

## Curriculum for the Higher Secondary Education

### Core Subjects

- Mother's tongue
- Hindi (for non-Hindi students) or elementary English or advanced English or any modern federal language or foreign language other than English or any classical language.
- Social science (for first two years only)
- Mathematics and general science (for first two years only)
- Any vocational subjects from the following: Spinning & weaving, metalwork, woodwork, gardening, handicraft, sewing & embroidery, printing, or typography.

**Optional Subjects**: The commission divided optional subjects into seven categories & fixed different curricula for each category.

- **Science:** Physics, chemistry, biology, geography, mathematics, physiology & hygiene.

- **Commerce:** Bookkeeping, shorthand and typing, commercial geography, and elements of economics.
- **Humanities:** History, geography, general principles of economics & civics, psychology & logic, mathematics, music, home science, classical language.
- **Technical:** Mechanical engineering, electrical engineering, general science, general mathematics & geometrical drawing.
- **Agriculture:** Animal husbandry, gardening, agricultural chemistry & botany.
- **Fine Arts:** Painting, modelling, music, dance, history of art, drawing & designing.
- **Home Science (Only for Girls):** Home economics, food, nutrition & cooking, motherhood (nursing & child care), home management.

The Report of Secondary Education Commission is genuinely called as "Bible for teachers" and is a landmark in the development of education in India. Despite its various drawbacks, the commission has paved the golden way to improve the secondary education system in India.

## NATIONAL COMMITTEE ON WOMEN'S EDUCATION, 1958 (DURGABAI DESHMUKH COMMITTEE)

The Educational Panel of the Planning Commission, in July 1957, recommended that "a suitable Committee should be appointed to go into the various aspects of the question relating to the nature of education for girls at the elementary, secondary and adult stages and to examine whether the present system was helping them to lead a happier and more useful life" The Conference of the State Education Ministers in 1957 also suggested that a special committee should be appointed to examine the whole question of women's education. National Committee on Women's Education was set up by the Government in May 1958, with Shrimati Durgabai Deshmukh as its Chairperson. The highest priority should be given to establishing parity between the education of boys and girls. The Centre and the States should make a bold and determined effort to face the difficulties and magnitude of the problem.

## Terms of References

- To suggest special measures to develop women's education at the primary and secondary levels.
- To examine the problem of wastage in girls' education at these levels.
- To survey the nature and extent of material and other facilities offered by voluntary welfare organizations for women's education.

## Recommendations of the Committee

- Joint Educational Adviser at the Centre should look after the education of girls and women.
- Concession in kind (not in cash) should be given to all girls of parents below a certain income level.
- The State government should establish State Councils for the education of girls and women.
- The University Grants Commission, a statutory body empowered to deal with colleges and universities, should provide a special fund of not less than Rs 1 crore for giving necessary grants to colleges to construct hostels for girls.
- More and more co-educational institutions should be started at the middle stage.
- Free education up to the middle stage.
- Suitable hostel facilities should be provided.
- Mid-day meals should be provided to all pupils of primary school

# THE EDUCATION COMMISSION (1964-66) / KOTHARI COMMISSION

The Kothari Commission (1964-66) was formed under the Chairmanship of **Dr DS Kothari** to formulate a coherent education policy for India, drawing on Nehru's Mission and articulating most of his main themes. The Commission was beneficial. It was comprehensive in scope, covering almost every aspect of the educational system. Unlike Commissions that focus on a single issue, it does not restrict themselves to just one. The following are two of the Report's standout features: (1) its comprehensive approach to educational reconstruction; (2) it attempts to project a blueprint of a national education system for India. According to the Commission, education was supposed to increase productivity, grow social and national unity, consolidate democracy, modernize the country, and develop social, moral, and spiritual values. Throughout the article, the importance of education in national growth is discussed in great detail. "Education and National Development" is an apt title. The Commission established three critical elements that would result in the desired educational outcome: (a) internal transformation to relate it to the life needs and aspirations of the nation; (b) qualitative improvement so that the standards achieved are adequate and become internationally comparable; (c) expansion of educational facilities broadly based on human resources needs, emphasizing equalization of education opportunities. It proposed that education be restructured into a standardized 10+2+3 pattern. It took a "manpower approach" to the enrolment issue, declaring that the primary goal of higher education was to meet the needs of industry and commerce. Even as it recognized its role in fostering social change, it criticized other sectors.

## Major Recommendations

- Education for accelerating process of modernization
- Adopting new methods of teaching
- Development of attitudes, values, and essential skills like Self study
- Educating people of all strata of society.
- Emphasizing teaching of vocational subjects and science.
- Establishing universities of excellence in the country.

## Educating for promoting social and national integration

- Introducing common school system of public education
- Developing all modern Indian languages
- Taking steps to enrich Hindi as quickly as possible.
- Encouraging and enabling students to participate in community living.

## Educating for Inculcation of National Values

- Introducing moral, social, and spiritual values.
- Providing syllabus giving information about religions of the world.
- Encouraging students to meet in groups for silent meditation.
- Presenting before student's high ideals of social justice and social service. Educating for the inculcation of national values

## NATIONAL EDUCATION POLICY (1968)

The government of India has formulated the National Education Policy (1968) to promote education amongst India's people. The policy covers basic education to colleges in both rural and urban India. The first National Policy on Education was broadcast in 1968 by the government of Prime Minister Indira Gandhi, the second Prime Minister Rajiv Gandhi in 1986, and then in Prime Minister Manmohan Singh. By the recommendations of this Committee, the 1968 National Education Policy was formulated. The most crucial development in improving the education sector was the national education policy in 1968. Education perspectives have been directed to all sectors of society to achieve the goal of harmony and integration. The use of regional languages in secondary schools was encouraged to establish an effective relationship between teachers and pupils. Excellence was given to Indians as a means of education in schools. There was a sense that education had the potential to act as a popular tool for social, economic, and political change. Educational objectives are instead linked to long-term national aspirations. In addition, the government has established committees to study the development of modern-day education, especially since independence, has concluded that Indian education requires radical reconstruction, almost a revolution. Goals and deal with the various problems facing the country. The 1979 National Education Policy Project proposed developing an education system that helps people improve their knowledge and academic skills. There has been a paradigm shift in government methodology. The main aim was to educate students about ethics and ethics to develop a good personality and become deserving citizens. It was suggested that an excellent educational system should be designed to promote constitutional values.

## Key highlights of NEP 1968

- Compulsory education for all children up to the age of 14, as specified by the Constitution of India.
- Better training and qualification of teachers.
- Pay more attention to the learning of regional languages, outlining the "three-language formula" to be applied in secondary education, and that was: 1. Hindi 2. English 3. Regional Language
- Since Hindi was adopted as the national language, the policy put wait on learning Hindi to promote Hindi as a common language for all Indians.
- The policy also stimulated learning the ancient Sanskrit language, an essential part of India's culture and heritage.
- The NEP of 1968 includes Work- Experience and National Service.

## NATIONAL EDUCATION POLICY (1986)

The National Education Policy of 1986 emphasized scholarships for the poor, adult education, reorientation of the system to promote gender equality, employment of teachers from oppressed groups and disabled persons. Physical and mental health and areas requiring special attention. Unique and also the development of new schools and universities. After independence, all these political initiatives have produced significant results in all areas, such as school enrolment, increased spending on education, growth in literacy rates, the universalization of education, etc.' NEP 1986 submitted proposals in various parts, viz.

- **Introductory:** It pointed out the significant contribution of NEP 1968
- **Essence and Role of Education:** It suggested the importance of education's role in one's life.
- **National System of Education**: It insisted on the principle on which NEP was conceived of First ten years in 10+2+3 pattern will have five years of primary education. The +2 will be a part of the school of education. Based on National Curriculum Framework Recommendations given by NEP 1986.

- **Education for Equality**: Education for women's equality. Education for SCs and STs. Other educational backward sections and areas-Minorites, Handicapped and Adult education **Reorganisation of Education at different stages:** Early Childhood Care and Education (ECCE) - Child-oriented approach. Focus on play and individuality of a child instead of formal methods of teaching 3Rs. Secondary Education Stage - Children with a unique talent and aptitude to be provided with opportunities to study at a faster pace Recommendations given by NEP 1986.
- **Pacesetting Residential Schools:** Navodaya Vidyalayas serves the objective of excellence, equity, and social justice to promote national integration by providing opportunities to talented children from different parts of the country to live and learn together.
- **Vocationalisation Stage:** Vocational courses or institutes will be the responsibility of the state.
- **Higher Education Stage**: Protect from degradation, Linguistic competency, High quality in research.

## RAMAMURTI REVIEW COMMITTEE (1990)

Acharya Ramamurti headed the review committee of 1990, popularly known as Ramamurti Review Committee., for evaluating the progress of the National Education Policy 1986. The major recommendations of Ramamurti review committee consist:

- **Development of a common school system:** Securing equity and social justice in education is the functioning of a common school system.
- **Removing disparities in education:** The need of the hour is planning for and implementing educational development programs in terms of disintegrated targets, area, community, and gender-specific activities.
- **Promotion of women's education:** An integrated approach in designing and implementing the schemes to promote the participation of the girls and women in education at all levels
- **Value education:** Value education is to be conceived as a continuous process. Value education should ensure that

education does not alienate the students from the family, community, and life.

- **Early childhood care and education:** The scope of the constitutional Directive (Article 45) should be enlarged to include ECCE.
- **Right to education:** The right to Education should be examined for inclusion among the fundamental rights.
- **Operation Blackboard:** The state governments should develop all decision-making power concerning the operation blackboard for planning and implementing the scheme.
- **Navodaya Vidyalayas:** No further Navodaya Vidyalaya needs to be opened. All the existing 261 Navodaya Vidyalayas may be transferred to the state sector. Navodaya Vidyalaya program of broad-based talent nurturing and pace-setting (A Day school each under the Common School system can function in the premises of Navodaya Vidyalayas).
- **Work experiences/ SUPW:** Work experience or socially useful Productive Work should be integrally linked with various subjects both at content and pedagogy.
- **Resources for education:** The first step should be to provide at least 6% of the GNP for schooling. All technical and professional education should be made self-financing.

## JANARDHANA REDDY COMMITTEE 1992 / CABE COMMITTEE 1992

The CABE committee was appointed under the chairmanship of Sri. Janardhana Reddy, on 31st July 1991, reviewed the implementation of the various parameters of NPE, taking into consideration the report of the Ramamurti Review Committee. The recommendations of the Committee consist:

- **Common School system**: Adequate measures need to be taken to implement the provision of NPE regarding the common school system. Disparities between schools should be ended as early as possible by upgrading the quality of ordinary schools and providing amenities for achieving minimum levels of learning.
- **Navodaya Vidyalayas**: The scheme should continue, and

a Navodaya Vidyalaya should be set up in each district. Constant review to keep the scheme as cost-effective as possible. Ensuring the continued validity and reliability of the admission tests. Periodic evaluation and appropriate modification of admission procedure. More particular attention to the pace-setting role of these institutions.

- **ECCE**: The scope of Article 45 of the constitution need not be enlarged. The Anganwadi workers should play an expanded role in several activities. Support services for women and children include childcare, family welfare, nutrition, and health.
- **Universalisation of Elementary Education:** Being one of the priorities strategies for UEE, Operation Blackboard should continue during the 7th plan in an expanded and extended form.
- **Adult and continuing education:** The 'dual-track approach' of simultaneously promoting UEE and adult literacy should continue in educational planning. Programs of post-literacy and continuing education should be planned for neo-literates.
- **Secondary Education:** Secondary education facilities all over the country. Open learning should be given.
- **Vocationalisation of Education:** Vocational stream at the +2 level. The work experience program should have a practical orientation about various subjects.
- **Management of Education:** The District Board of Education should be set up. "Making the system work" and Formulation and Implementation of an Action Plan.
- **Resources for Education:** Need-based financing has to be provided for priority areas. Revising the fee structure with appropriate support to needy students through student loans.

## YASH PAL COMMITTEE REPORT, 1993 / LEARNING WITHOUT BURDEN

Yash Pal Committee proposed the 'Learning without Burden' (1993), which states that learning has become a burden and stress for children and their parents. To have a fresh look at the problems of education, particularly regarding the issue of an academic burden on students, the Ministry of Human Resource Development, Government of India, set up a National Advisory Committee in March 1992. The National Advisory Committee presented its report entitled, *Learning Without Burden* on 15th July 1993.

**Terms of References**: (a) To advise on the ways and means to reduce the load on school students at all levels, particularly the young students, while improving quality of learning, including the capability for life-long self-learning and skill formulation. (b) In doing this, the Committee may examine all aspects of curricula, entrance criteria, and exit attainments at various levels and examine the impact of examinations, admissions to higher education institutions, and professional courses.

## Recommendations of the Committee

- In the Final Report submitted by the committee to the Ministry of Human Resource Development (MHRD), it was recommended that the deemed university status should be abandoned.
- All the deserving deemed universities should be either converted to full-fledged universities or would have to be scrapped.
- A GRE like test needs to be evolved for the purpose of university education.
- A Commission must replace NCTE, AICTE, UGC, and others for Higher Education and Research (CHER) – a seven-member body. This new regulator must be free from political pressures.
- The process of framing the curriculum and writing textbooks should be decentralized and involve more teachers.
- Education committees should be constituted at the village, block, and district levels.
- The jurisdiction of CBSE should be restricted to KVs and the Navodaya Vidyalayas only, and all other schools should be affiliated with the respective state boards.
- Interview tests and interviews for nursery admissions should be done away with.

- The norms for giving private schools recognition need to be more stringent to avoid commercialization.
- There should be no compulsion for school children to carry heavy books to school.
- Primary school children should not be given any homework. And even for the higher classes, it should be non-textual.
- The teacher-pupil ratio should be reduced to at least 1:30. Further recommended the greater use of electronic media. It also recommended many steps for improving teacher training.

In short, before 1947, the role of educational administrators in India was simply to carry out the restricted educational programme developed by the British. We have developed vastly expanded educational programmes following independence with considerably changed objectives; for implementing these new programmes, the academic administrator's job takes on new dimensions and requires new theories of school administration and new techniques. A series of commissions and committees were appointed to survey, study, review and recommend improvements in the different education sectors to improve the quality of education. The Commission and Policies related education has from time-to-time sought guidance from the Constitution vision of India as a secular, egalitarian and pluralistic society, founded on the values of social justice and equality. Education has derived its content and meaning from the Constitution, and the system has tried to democratize opportunities to move in the direction of education. Education and skill development have a significant role in the larger human capital domain. There is a lot of room for improvement.

## ISSUES, PROBLEMS AND REMEDIAL MEASURES OF PRIMARY EDUCATION IN KERALA

Primary education is a stage of formal education that comes after pre-school and before secondary school. It is also called elementary education. It is the foundation for secondary education and tertiary education as well as lifelong education. There are mainly four streams in school education in India- Preschool, Primary, Secondary, Higher Secondary. The International Standard Classification of Education considers primary education as a single-phase where programmes are typically designed to provide fundamental skills in reading, writing and mathematics and to establish a solid foundation for learning. The United Nations Children's Fund (UNICEF), believes that providing children with primary education has many positive effects. It (a) Decreases poverty, (b) Decreases child mortality rates, (c) Encourages gender equality, and (d) Increases environmental understanding.

## Primary Education in India after Independence

With the introduction of Five-year plans, began the plan of aiming to achieve Universalisation of Elementary Education (UEE). The first five-year plan (1951-1956) aimed to achieve 60% enrolment of those aged up to 11 years from the 40% enrolment in 1950. From then onwards India is trying hard to attain Universalisation of Elementary Education. As of now, UEE is to be achieved by 2030 as suggested by the NPE 2019. The various Education Commissions and Policies introduced over the years too, recommended for the enhancement of primary education.

## Recommendations of Educational Commissions on Primary Education and Acts

Taking into consideration the recommendations of various commissions of education in India after Independence, it is found that the two commissions, viz. University Education Commission and Secondary Education Commission, prior to Kothari commission did not mention anything about primary education. It is in the recommendations of Kothari Commission, that primary education is seen mentioned. A brief view of the Kothari Commission is given below:

### Indian Education Commission/Kothari Commission 1964-66

The Indian Education Commission popularly known as the Kothari Commission (1964-66) was set up by the government of India on 14th July, 1964, under the chairmanship of Dr Daulat Singh Kothari. The objective of the Kothari Education Commission (1964-66) was to examine the different aspects of the education system in India. Recommendations of the Commission with regard to Primary Education are:

- **Provision for free and compulsory Education:** The Kothari commission recommended for early fulfilment of the

Directive Principles of State Policy (DPSP) of India under article 45 of the Indian Constitution, which aimed to provide free and compulsory education for children between 6 to 14 years. It aimed to increase enrolment in schools to attend the desirable goal of free and compulsory education.

- **Status, Emoluments and Education of Teachers:** The teacher is undoubtedly a necessary factor in determining the quality of education and its contribution to national development It is the teacher's personal qualities and character, educational qualifications and professional competence that the success of all educational endeavour must ultimately depend. Teachers must be accorded an honoured place in society. Their emoluments and other service conditions should be adequate and satisfactory, having regard to their qualifications and responsibilities. The academic freedom of teachers to pursue and publish independent studies and researches and to speak and write about significant national and international issues should be protected. Teacher education, particularly in-service education, should receive due emphasis.
- **Development of languages:** (a) Importance for regional languages: The Commission recognized the importance of Indian language and literature for the educational and cultural development of Indians. It intended to spread knowledge through regional languages and to reduce the gap between the intelligentsia and the common people. It recommended taking urgent steps to promote regional language as a medium of instruction at the University level also. Instruction in primary and secondary education were already in regional language. (b) Three language formula: The Kothari commission recommended for the adoption of three language formula by the state governments at the secondary level. It intended to promote a modern Indian language, which was preferably to be any South Indian language apart from Hindi and English in the Hindi speaking States. Hindi and English along with the regional language were to be the part of the non-Hindi speaking states in India. Hindi was intended to be developed as a link language and as a medium of expression for the composite culture of India. (c) Sanskrit and international

language: The commission recognized the importance of Sanskrit in the growth and development of Indian languages and its contribution to the cultural unity of the country. Therefore, the Commission recommended exploring the possibility of including Sanskrit for the study of Indian languages, History, Ideology and Indian philosophy, etc. The Commission emphasized the need to study international languages especially English in India. This was also aimed to promote study in science and technology in India.

- **Recommendation on the Educational Structure in India:** The committee highlighted the advantages of a uniform educational structure throughout the country. It recommended 10 + 2 + 3 as the pattern of educational structure in the country. Recommended increase in the Government's expenditure on education. The commission highlighted the need to increase the investment in education to reach a level of 6% of national expenditure on education.
- **Coordination between the Centre and the states:** The need for coordination between the states and the central government was also necessary for the development of education.
- **Equalization of Educational Opportunity:** Strenuous efforts should be made to equalize educational opportunity. (a) Regional imbalances in the provision of educational facilities should be corrected and good educational facilities should be provided in rural and other backward areas. (b) To promote social cohesion and national integration the Common School System as recommended by the Education Commission should be adopted. Efforts should be made to improve the standard of education in general schools. All special schools like Public Schools should be required to admit students on the basis of merit and also to provide a prescribed proportion of free studentships to prevent segregation of social classes. This will not, however, affect the rights of minorities under Article 30 of the Constitution. (c) The education of girls should receive emphasis, not only on grounds of social justice, but also because it accelerates social transformation. (d) More intensive efforts are needed to develop education among the backward classes and especially among the tribal people.

(e) Educational facilities for the physically and mentally handicapped children should be expanded and attempts should be made to develop integrated programs enabling the handicapped children to study in regular schools.

- **Identification of Talent:** For the cultivation of excellence, it is necessary that talent in diverse fields should be identified at an early age as possible, and every opportunity may be provided for its full development.
- **Work-experience and National Service:** The school and the community should be brought closer through suitable programs of mutual service and support. Work-experience and national service, including participation in meaningful and challenging programs of community service and national reconstruction, should accordingly become an integral part of education. Emphasis in these programs should be on self-help, character formation and on developing a sense of social commitment.
- **Science Education and Research:** With a view to accelerating the growth of the national economy, Science education and Research should receive high priority. Science and Mathematics should be an integral part of general education till the end of the school stage.
- **Education for Agriculture and Industry:** Special emphasis should be placed on the development of education for agriculture and industry. (a) In technical education, practical training in industry should form an integral part of such education. Technical education and research should be related closely to industry, encouraging the flow of personnel both ways and providing for continuous cooperation in the provision, design and periodical review of training programs and facilities. (b) There should be a continuous review of the agricultural, industrial and other technical manpower needs of the country and efforts should be made continuously to maintain a proper balance between the output of the educational institutions and employment opportunities.
- **Production of Books:** The quality of books should be improved by attracting the best writing talent through a liberal policy of incentives and remuneration. Immediate steps

should be taken for the production of high-quality textbooks for schools and universities. Frequent changes of textbooks should be avoided and their prices should be low enough for students of ordinary means to buy them. The possibility of establishing autonomous book corporations on commercial lines should be examined and efforts should be made to have a few basic textbooks common throughout the country. Special attention should be given to books for children and to university- level books in regional languages.

- **Examinations:** A major goal of examination reforms should be to improve the reliability and validity of examinations and to make evaluation a continuous process aimed at helping the student to improve his level of achievement rather than at 'certifying' the quality of his performance at a given moment of time.

In short, Indian Education Commission/Kothari Commission 1964-66 not much is said about primary education with regard to this commission, as it is aimed at examining all aspects of the educational sector across the country.

## ACTS RELATED TO PRIMARY EDUCATION

**Right to Education Act (RTE) 2009:** Right to Education Act (RTE) helps to provide free and compulsory education to children. In 2009, it was enforced as a fundamental right under Article 21-A. The Right to Education serves as a building block to ensure that every child has his or her right to get a quality elementary education.

**Constitutional Background:** Originally Part IV of Indian Constitution, Article 45 and Article 39 (f) had a provision for state funded as well as equitable and accessible education. The first official document on the Right to Education was Ramamurti Committee Report in 1990. In 1993, the Supreme Court's landmark judgment in the Unnikrishnan J.P. vs State of Andhra Pradesh and Others held that Education is a Fundamental right flowing from Article 21. Tapas Majumdar Committee (1999) was set up, which encompassed insertion of Article 21A. The 86th amendment to the constitution of India in 2002, provided Right to Education as a fundamental right in part-III of the Constitution. The same amendment inserted Article 21A which made Right to Education a fundamental right for children between

6-14 years. The 86th amendment provided for a follow-up legislation for Right to Education Bill 2008 and finally Right to Education Act 2009.

**Features of Right to Education (RTE) Act, 2009:** The RTE Act aims to provide primary education to all children aged 6 to 14 years. It enforces Education as a Fundamental Right (Article 21). The act mandates 25% reservation for disadvantaged sections of the society where disadvantaged groups include: a) SCs and STs, b) Socially Backward Class, c) Differently abled. It also makes provisions for a non-admitted child to be admitted to an age-appropriate class. It also states that sharing of financial and other responsibilities between the Central and State Governments. It lays down the norms and standards related to: a) Pupil Teacher Ratios (PTRs), b) Buildings and infrastructure, c) School-working days, d) Teacher-working hours. It had a clause for "No Detention Policy" which has been removed under The Right of children to free and compulsory education Act, 2019. It also provides for prohibition of deployment of teachers for noneducational work, other than decennial census, elections to local authority, state legislatures and parliament, and disaster relief. It provides for the appointment of teachers with the requisite entry and academic qualifications. It prohibits: a) Physical punishment and mental harassment, b) Screening procedures for admission of children, c) Capitation fee, d) Private tuition by teachers, e) Running of schools without recognition. It focuses on making the child free of fear, trauma and anxiety through a system of child friendly and child centred learning.

## Achievements of Right to Education Act, 2009

- The RTE Act has successfully managed to increase enrolment in the upper primary level (Class 6-8).
- Stricter infrastructure norms resulted in improved school infrastructure, especially in rural areas.
- More than 3.3 million students secured admission under 25% quota norm under RTE.
- It made education inclusive and accessible nationwide.
- Removal of "no detention policy" has brought accountability in the elementary education system.

**Limitation of Right to Education Act, 2009**

- Age group for which Right to Education is available ranges from 6 – 14 years of age only, which can be made more inclusive and encompassing by expanding it to 0 – 18 years.
- There is no focus on quality of learning, as shown by multiple ASER (Annual Status of Education Reports) reports, thus RTE Act appears to be mostly input oriented.
- Five States namely Goa, Manipur, Mizoram, Sikkim and Telangana have not even issued notification regarding 25% seats for underprivileged children of society under the RTE. More focus is being given over statistics of RTE rather than quality of learning.
- Lack of teachers affect pupil-teacher ratio mandated by RTE which in turn affects the quality of teaching.

## IMPLEMENTATION OF VARIOUS PROGRAMMES FOR ATTAINING UNIVERSALISATION OF ELEMENTARY EDUCATION

The scheme of Operation Blackboard was launched in 1987 in pursuance of NPE-POA, to provide minimum essential facilities to all primary schools in India.

### Operation Blackboard

Operation Blackboard is a centrally sponsored programme which was started in 1987 immediately after the National Policy on Education of 1986 was released to supply the bare minimum crucial facilities to all primary schools in the country. The major policy plank to improve school quality was Operation Blackboard, a centrally sponsored scheme which laid down, for the first time, the minimum criteria of a primary school: two rooms, two teachers (one of them preferably female), and a set of 'minimum essential' teaching learning aids (TLA). The Salient features of Operation Blackboard which started in 1987 are:

- To supply bare minimum important facilities to all the primary schools in the country.
- To provide necessary institutional equipment and instructional material to the students studying in primary setup.

- To provide salary for an additional teacher if enrolment is more than 100 students.
- All the teachers will be trained under exclusively designed teacher preparation program.
- The replacement facility for broken and non-functioning materials.
- Leverage in purchasing teaching aids and additional items as requisite for local needs.
- 50% of teachers should be female to encourage girl child admissions.
- The school building will be designed as per the local needs.
- The central and state governments should provide funds for the school equipment and building.

Implementation of NPE 1986 initiates for Universalisation of Elementary Education in the form of major Central government programmes made an impressive beginning but faced serious disruption with the launch of DPEP in 1994, a programme that came with structural adjustment policies and acceptance of external funding, including a loan from the World Bank.

## District Primary Education Project (DPEP)

The programme began in 42 districts in 1994, spreading over seven states and expanded in a phased manner to cover around 275 districts. The main objectives of DPEP were: (a) all children to be in schools, Education Guarantee Scheme Centres, Alternative Schools, 'Back-to-School' camps by 2003; (b) all children complete five years of primary schooling by 2007; (c) all children complete eight years of elementary schooling by 2010; (d) focus on elementary education of satisfactory quality with emphasis on education for life; (e) bridge all gender and social category gaps at the primary stage by 2007 and, at the upper primary level, by 2010; and (f) universal retention by 2010. In fact, the SSA package looked more like extension of DPEP template to all the districts of the country under the same model of dual governance system at the State level. Fragmented approach to dealing with UEE, with focus only on five years of schooling, and a fractured framework, dividing the country vertically as DPEP and non-DPEP districts, distorted the national perspective as well as the role of State

Governments in moving towards the goal of UEE. With the launch of Sarva Shiksha Abhiyan (SSA) in 2001, national targets, timelines, strategies and programmes returned to the planning table. In a way, SSA marked the revival and reconstruction of the national perspective as it stitched together a national programme encompassing the whole country and subsuming all national initiatives related to UEE under an umbrella Centrally Sponsored Scheme. SSA also took forward the steps initiated after NPE 1986 for increased involvement of Central Government in UEE. In fact, as SSA grew in size and coverage and, in particular, with SSA being declared as the main instrumentality for implementing the RTE, UEE has largely become a Central subject complete with programme and financing norms in great detail, leaving only implementation management to the State Governments.

## Sarva Shiksha Abhiyan 2000-2001

Sarva Shiksha Abhiyan (SSA) is Government of India's flagship programme for achievement of Universalization of Elementary Education (UEE) in a time bound manner, as mandated by 86th amendment to the Constitution of India making free and compulsory Education to the Children of 6-14 years age group, a Fundamental Right. SSA was being implemented in partnership with State Governments to cover the entire country and address the needs of 192 million children in 1.1 million habitations. The programme seeks to open new schools in those habitations which do not have schooling facilities and strengthen existing school infrastructure through provision of additional class rooms, toilets, drinking water, maintenance grant and school improvement grants. Existing schools with inadequate teacher strength are provided with additional teachers, while the capacity of existing teachers is being strengthened by extensive training, grants for developing teaching-learning materials and strengthening of the academic support structure- at a cluster, block and district level. SSA seeks to provide quality elementary education including life skills. SSA has a special focus on girl's education and children with special needs. SSA also seeks to provide computer education to bridge the digital divide. However, unfortunately, SSA took shape under the shadow of the previous decade, adopting many of the same ill-conceived strategies. Despite heightened public consciousness and increased civil society involvement, SSA seemed to be struggling to regain people's trust in the public system of education. This, at least in part, has led to the unprecedented growth of private self-financing schools and apparent migration of children from Government to private schools. The resulting impact has been the deepening as well as widening of inequity across the system within both public and private initiatives, thereby denting the progress of universal free and compulsory education as mandated by the Constitution.

## Samagra Shiksha Abhiyan 2018-19

The Union Budget, 2018-19, has proposed to treat school education holistically without segmentation from pre-primary to Class 12. Samagra Shiksha – an overarching programme for the school education sector extending from preschool to class 12 has been, therefore, prepared with the broader goal of improving school effectiveness measured in terms of equal opportunities for schooling and equitable learning outcomes. It subsumes the three erstwhile schemes of Sarva Shiksha Abhiyan (SSA), Rashtriya Madhyamik Shiksha Abhiyan (RMSA) and Teacher Education (TE). This sector-wide development programme/ scheme would also help harmonise the implementation mechanisms and transaction costs at all levels, particularly in using state, district and sub-district level systems and resources, besides envisaging one comprehensive strategic plan for development of school education at the district level. The shift in the focus is from project objectives to improving systems level performance and schooling outcomes which will be the emphasis of the combined scheme along-with incentivizing states towards improving quality of education.

## ISSUES AND PROBLEMS IN THE EDUCATION IN KERALA

The Kerala Model of Development has been much acclaimed for its attainment with the limited resources of a high quality of life index comparable to that of the developed countries. Kerala stands ahead of other states in the Human Development Index (HDI) list estimated for the various states in India. The educational scenario in Kerala is far advanced than other states in India. The Kerala model of development over it attributed success to the achievements in the area of education and health. Most of the changes and developments in the field of education have occurred since independence. Kerala continues to be a top achiever in composite ranking of primary and upper primary education, according to the new statistics released by the Central Government. In 1991 the state could declare its commitment to education by declaring it as the first complete literate state. In 2016 Vice President of India declared Kerala as the first Indian State to achieve total primary education.

In spite of the large number of educational institutions in the state, the quality of education at all levels in Kerala has been showing a decline due to financial constraints resulting from a quantitative expansion of the sector. A study published in 1999 by the Centre for Socio-economic and Environmental Studies states that while the dropout rates are very low in primary schools, the same increases in the ninth and the tenth standards in Kerala. This is particularly true of SC/ST students. Schools showed that only 73% of the students joining at 1st Standard reach the 10th Standard. In the case of scheduled caste students, only 59% reach the 10th standard. 60% of Scheduled Tribal students drop out by the 10th standard. Kerala has made major achievements in school enrolment at the primary level and in preventing drop outs, because of the pioneering government funded programmes like Noon Meal Scheme. But even in the case of discontinuation rates of the children in the age group 6-14 years, the position of SC/ST students is higher than their counterparts in states like Bihar, Uttar Pradesh, Himachal Pradesh, Rajasthan and North-Eastern region. Some of the qualitative aspects of Kerala's primary education are equally distressing. This is despite the fact that the annual household expenditure on elementary education per student is one of the highest in the country (Rs. 586 in Kerala as against Rs. 378 at the national level). A study by the NCERT showed that Kerala ranked very low among the Indian states in terms of learning achievement of primary school children. About 30 per cent of the children who complete primary school do not reach the necessary achievement levels in literacy and numeracy. The NCERT study comes to the conclusion that serious measures are called for to improve the teaching/learning process in order to enhance learner achievements. Although the achievements in terms of expansion of schools and enrolment are impressive, many of the schools do not have adequate infrastructural facilities. Many of them are run in old dilapidated buildings and thatched sheds. Many of them lack even drinking water facilities, latrines and urinals.

## Remedial Measures:

The policies followed by the successive governments in Kerala made formal education more accessible to its common folk. Some of the major initiatives taken include:

- providing text books at low prices
- withdrawing tuition fee
- allowing concessional rate for students' conveyance
- providing free lunch in schools
- ensuring at least one high school in every panchayath
- adopting new approach promotions to higher classes
- expanding vocational and technical education
- taking steps for ensuring higher secondary education for all
- bringing higher secondary within the fold of school education
- envisioning IT as a part of the curriculum
- launching of EDUSAT and VICTERS channels
- strengthening the school library system.

Thus, the efforts of various governments in Kerala have enhanced the educational opportunities in the state. Today, there is at least one lower primary school in a radius of one kilometre, one upper primary school in a radius of three kilometres and a high school each in a range of four kilometres.

## Innovations in curriculum development and evaluation in primary education

In 2001, Kerala launched a unique project titled IT@school after having identified the potential of using Information Technology in enhancing the quality of education in the State. The objective of the project is to enhance the intellectual capability of teachers and the curricular comprehension of the students by providing ICT enabled education. In the first phase of the project, IT was taught only as a subject. But in the second phase, IT was a part of education used in transacting the various subjects taught in school like science, mathematics, humanities and languages. The Kerala Infrastructure and Technology for Education (KITE) was the implementing agency of the Hi-tec school programme. Each Hi-Tech classroom is equipped with Laptop, ceiling mounted Multimedia Projector, Whiteboard / Projection

Screen, USB Speakers, High Speed Broadband internet and access to Samagra Resource Portal. The Hi-Tech IT Labs feature Laptops, Sound system and Multifunction Printers. Schools are provided with a 42-inch LED TV, Full HD webcam and a DSLR Camera. Teachers were trained to conduct ICT enabled classes. The ICT enabled classes are conducted using Samagra portal.

## Samagra

SAMAGRA, is a repository of digital resources of all subjects from Class 1 to 12 in the form of videos, animations, audios, stimulations, interactive contents, pictures etc. Multiple levels of log-ins are integrated in SAMAGRA for the Teachers, Public and Administrators. Teachers contribute various learning resources such as a video, images, interactive like pdb, ggb, swf, gif and the students are able to access these contents without any restriction. It also enables the unit plan of every chapter in addition to micro planning. All e-Resources available in SAMAGRA can be downloaded from anywhere. The portal also features specific Forums for discussions, in which teachers can clarify the doubts irrespective of location constraints. It also has e-Textbooks of all subjects in four mediums viz Malayalam, English, Tamil and Kannada. This enables the students to study the subjects even in the absence of physical textbooks.

## Samagra Shiksha, Kerala (SSK)

Samagra Shiksha, Kerala, Integrated scheme for school education, came in to force on November 1 st 2018. Sarva Shiksha Abhiyan and Rashtriya Madhyamik Shiksha Abhiyan were merged to form Samagra Shiksha, Kerala. Samagra Shiksha envisages the 'school' as a continuum from pre-school, primary, upper primary, secondary to senior secondary levels. The vision of the Scheme is to ensure inclusive and equitable quality education from pre-school to senior secondary stage in accordance with the Sustainable Development Goal (SDG) for Education. General education department and Samagra Shiksha, Kerala have initiated various schemes in the field of education to increase the enrolment of students in public schools and to enhance the quality of student learning. The **major objectives of the SSK** include:

- provision of quality education and enhancing learning outcomes of students;

- bridging social and gender gaps in school education;
- ensuring equity and inclusion at all levels of school education;
- ensuring minimum standards in schooling provision;
- promoting vocationalisation of education;
- support states in implementation of right of children to free and compulsory education RTE Act, 2009; and
- strengthening and up-gradation of SCERTs / State Institutes of Education and DIET as a nodal agency for teacher training.

The main outcomes of the Scheme are envisaged as Universal Access, Equity and Quality, promoting vocationalisation of education and strengthening of Teacher Education Institutions (TEIs).

## Curriculum Development in Primary Education under SSK

Some important aspects of curriculum development in primary education include:

- Development of curriculum document and materials
- Development of Technical Dictionary
- Curriculum approach paper
- Additional reading material (English, Arabic, Sanskrit, Urdu)
- Nurturing Mathematical Talents in Schools (NuMATS)
- Development of assessment tools and techniques
- Student Talent Enrichment Programme in Social Science (STEPS)
- Enhancement programme for boosting the talents of LSS and USS achievers.
- Programmes relating to continuous and Comprehensive Evaluation (Mentoring)
- Curriculum development for inclusive education

Besides developing curriculum for general education, the SCERT also develops curriculum for the children with special needs of Kerala. The project *Thuna* (companion) aims to solve the scholastic backwardness by identifying the students in the upper primary classes who are scholastically backward.

**Software for the Visually Impaired:** SCERT with the technical support of KELTRON developed a software for the Visual Impaired for typing in Malayalam, English Tamil, Kannada and Tamil called Sharadha Braille Writer using six keys of the computer keyboard.

**Curriculum for Hearing Impaired:** Based on the curriculum developed for the general schools, the curriculum has been adapted for the hearing impaired for the class V to X. Subsequently the adaptation has been made in the textbooks for all subjects which was reflected in the teacher's handbook. Based on the study conducted by the SCERT, a curriculum was developed for the Hearing Impaired at the Primary Level (ClassI-IV). An entry-level book (Malayalam, English and Mathematics) for Class 1 were also prepared as a preparatory programme.

**Curriculum for Intellectually challenged:** SCERT, Kerala conducted a Status Study of the Intellectually Challenged in Kerala and accordingly a unique curriculum was developed for the intellectually challenged at the primary level for children of age group 7-11. The package included 8 curriculum handbooks for teachers, eight workbooks for students and activity-based resource CD for the transaction of the books. The curriculum aims at developing different abilities, skills and attitudes; the activity package ensures full participation of students. Learning enhancement programmes like Hello English, Ganithavijayam, Malayalathilakam, Sureli Hindi, Sashtrammadhuram, Bhoumam are some unique programmes undertaken by Samagra Shiksha, Kerala in Primary Education.

**Evaluation in Primary Education:** Evaluation is widely acknowledged as a powerful means of improving the quality of education. It is one of the key components of any curriculum. It plays a vital role in teaching learning process and impacts the quality of teaching and learning. Only when learners are evaluated, can their weaknesses and difficulties be diagnosed and remedies be given for more effective learning. The introduction of Continuous and Comprehensive Evaluation (CCE) is considered as one of the major steps taken in this regard to improve and strengthen the quality of learner evaluation. The state of Kerala has been going through a series of educational reforms over a decade or more and the introduction of CCE in the state is one among them. As emphasized by Kerala Curriculum Framework (2007) the implementation of new evaluation practices focusing on CCE was introduced right from primary to secondary level in 2008. As majority of teachers were not familiar with the methods of CCE, serious practical problems came up in classrooms, especially at upper primary level. The SCERT organized a training program in three stages to address the issues and to give practical training on evaluation methods.

**Quality and Innovation in Primary Education:** Kerala is re-investing heavily in public education to ensure that its students are prepared for a changing world, equipped with knowledge, skills and values, which will help them to compete with fellow students from around the world. The watch word in Education for Kerala, is to 'move the pedagogy further' thus focusing on equitable quality. Samagra Shiksha, Kerala has not confined its scope of quality as one of the interventions, but has attempted to bring all interventions under the wide category of quality education. CCE has been implemented in all classes across different subjects. All round development of the child is ensured through curriculum revision, development of Activity books for Arts and Work Education and through appointment of specialist teachers in Work Education, Art Education and Physical education. Revision of text books has been undertaken by the state ensuring learning through activities, discovery and exploration, in a child friendly and child-centred manner. All round development of the child is ensured through curriculum revision, development of Activity books for Arts Education and Work Education, Health and Physical Education. State also appointed specialist teachers to teach Arts Education and Work Education, Health and Physical Education. From the above discussion, it is evident that the nature of primary education has changed from time to time. A journey of imparting primary education from the pre-independent period to present India had many versions to seen. Education is the birth right of child. Thus, the State shall make effort to provide elementary education to all children irrespective of caste, creed, sex, religion, socio-economic status and place of birth or living. Elementary education is no doubt of extreme importance, as everything a child learns in these early days is built on as they get older.

## CURRICULUM DEVELOPMENT

The word Curriculum was derived from the Latin word "currere" which means "course or track" to be followed. It is the sum total of all the experiences given to leaner under the protection of a school or university. It is also a vehicle for helping the learners in the journey of their attainment of educational goals, objectives and aims. It is systematic arrangements of all the selected experiences given to a leaner in the schools or colleges. Curriculum is cluster of all experiences given to a group of learners to attain the particular educational program. Curriculum frequently refers to the knowledge and skills which are expected to learn, it includes, the areas of leaning, objectives they are expected to attain, the matter of content and related work such as assignments projects the reference materials, videos, presentations and the reading used for a course and finally the evaluation process. Curriculum is means to attain the predetermined goals and objectives of the leaner and teachers. It includes curricular and co-curricular activities. From these interpretations we can understand that the curriculum must be creatively and carefully integrated or incorporated.

## Meaning and concept of curriculum development process

According to **Rogers and Taylor** Curriculum development describes all the ways in which teaching or training organization plans and guides learning. This learning can take place in groups or with individual learners. It can take place inside or outside the classroom. It can take place in an institutional setting like school, college, training centre, or in a village or a field. It is central to the teaching-learning process. Simply curriculum development means the process made for the development of curriculum. Curriculum development process takes place after the deep discussion made from subject experts, project managers instructional designer's writer's copy editors etc. An effective content is prepared by this panel of expert. It can be defined as arrangements or changes made for the creative improvements and developments of the course offered to higher education. The changes and improvements are made in the perspective of his/her research and professional development and thereby achieve the development of the society also. Curriculum development process systematically organizes to give clear picture of what to taught who will be taught and how it will be taught. There is an interrelation and coordination between each component of the curriculum. For example, when we select a topic any subject for giving a project, we will consider his/her age, family, society needs, resources available etc There must be a chain of developmental process to develop a society. First, the school curriculum, particularly in higher education, must be developed to preserve the country's national identity and to ensure its economy's growth and stability. Thus, the president of a country must have a clear vision for his people and the country as well. There must be a chain of developmental process to develop a society. First, the school curriculum, particularly in higher education, must be developed to preserve the country's national identity and to ensure its economy's growth and stability. Thus, the higher authority of a country must have a clear vision for his people and the country as well.

## Need and importance of curriculum development process

Curriculum development has wide scope because it is not only about the school, the learners, and the teachers. It is also about the development of society as a whole. The present economy is a type of knowledge economy. Curriculum development plays a vital role in improving the economy of a country. It also provides answers or solutions to the world's present conditions and problems, such as environment, politics, socio-economics, and other issues of poverty, climate change, and sustainable development. There must be a chain of developmental process to develop a society. First, the school curriculum, particularly in higher education, must be developed to preserve the country's national identity and to ensure its economy's growth and stability. Thus, the higher authority of education has a clear vision for his people and the country as well.

## Importance of curriculum development

- Curriculum development is a purposeful activity.
- It is undertaken to design or redesign for the realization of certain specific educational objectives.
- The curriculum is the root map for the journey of school or university education.
- The curriculum should be restructured and revised on a regular basis so that it is able serve the changing needs of, both students and society.

**Clear purpose and goals:** Curriculum development process provides written document revealing the curricular goals which are intended student development outcomes. These goals and objectives are specified in considerable detail and in language of common people.

**Continuous assessment and improvement of quality**: There must be valid and reliable assessment for the realization of the achievement of certain specific objectives. It should be reorganized or restructured periodically for the satisfaction of changing need of the society as whole.

**A rational sequence**: In curriculum educational activities are arranged in sequential order, in order to satisfy the developmental stages of the stake holders.

## Steps in curriculum development process

1. Gathering Information: The first step in the curriculum development process involves the collection of information about learner's attitude towards content, availability of material, the person who take the content, previous knowledge of the leaner etc. Instructional designers collect all these information from different sources and move to second step.
2. Design: Then the panel conduct the study about the information collected in the first step and stated the second step that is development of the content. Before design the content there need some clear objectives. They are; Identify, Modify, Plan, and Evaluate. After setting the objectives they carefully connect them to the content. They ensure whether the leaning outcomes can occur. They also examine the environment of the content used. The team collects information about the method used for delivery of content, the platform, whether it is digital or not, whether it can be used for further higher studies like research.
3. Building the Content: The third step of curriculum development process is to build the content into a transactional unit by adding required graphics, animations etc.
4. Evaluation and reporting: The final step of the curriculum development process is evaluation and reporting. This is an important step in the process of curriculum development, because the end results are revealing the evaluation process. For this formative and summative evaluation procedures are used.

It is a method for determining the quality and effectiveness of the implemented curriculum for the stake holders like learners, parents, teachers the society administrators, and the nation as a whole.

## Principles of Curriculum Construction

- **Principle of Child centeredness:** According to the new curriculum policy learners are the key factor of every curriculum. So, it should be prepared according to the wants and needs of the leaner. It facilitates them to determine their own learning following their natural curiosities, interests and passions. It should include the following principles: Play and Curiosity, Self-Discovery, The Whole Child, Choice and Consequences, Empathy, Caring, and Mutual Trust, Taking Reasonable Risks, Time for Solitude, Reflection, and a Sense of Wonder.
- **Principle of Flexibility and Variety:** The learners should be given freedom of choice in selecting subjects. The learners should not be compelled to take up a course of study under pressure. Local and individual differences among the students must be taken proper care, when the time of construction of curriculum. There must a variety in the structure of curriculum in order to cater the varying needs of the individual. The learners should give full freedom to select the subjects and should not be compelled to take the course he/she need.
- **Principle of correlation:** There must exist a correlation and coordination between the various subject selected with other subjects. It creates a smooth way for the journey of study.
- **Principle of integration:** The curriculum should integrate: (a) Cognitive, affective and psychomotor objectives and abilities, (b) Knowledge and experience, (c) Objectives and content, and (4) Child's activity and needs with the society needs and activity. It should be related to the social environment of the students. Here the equal/ balance importance should be given to the need of the Child and need of the Community. The principle of integration is an important principle in the development of curriculum. Principle of integration leads the all-round development of the individual. Variety of

subjects is included in the curriculum at a stage of education, so there should be integration with all subjected included the curriculum. For example, mathematics, science, history geography etc are included in one term or semester. So, there must keep the principle of integration.

- **Principle of community service:** As a social being the individual always interact with the society, so in the process of curriculum development the principle of community services must be followed. The modern curriculum fulfils the community needs of the individual. The curriculum should be designed as to satisfies the optimum use of community resources for the development of education and the vice versa.
- **Principle of Values:** In the changing world a number of desirable values are to be keeping with them. So modern curriculum provides appropriate values of social, moral spiritual, democratic and aesthetic. This principle helps them to identify the right and wrong activities in the society.
- **Principle of Totality:** From each situation of a leaner creates an environment for a bit of information for his educational purpose. So, the curriculum should also create such a situation. Curriculum should mould a leaner as a complete man in all stages of development. For example, physically, mentally, and morally. Thus, curriculum include all information to help them to become a complete man.

## Approaches to Curriculum Construction

The curriculum development experts may use one or more approaches in planning implementing and evaluating the curriculum Approaches used in curriculum development means that, the effective way or manner in which the experts arranged the whole experiences given to the learner. They are the different strategies applied in the curriculum content and learning activities are presented to the learner. Approaches to curriculum development can also be regarded as models of curriculum development. There are different approaches to curriculum development; viz. Child or leaner-centred, Subject centred, Problem centred and human relation centred. The **child centred approach** is based on the principle of the child is key factor of the educational process. That means the curriculum is framed based on the need's abilities, knowledge, skill, purpose of the leaner. The **Subject centred approach** means the curriculum design prescribes different and separate subjects into one broad field. The **Problem centred approach** means that the curriculum is designed on the basis of problems faced by the leaner in the future life and build the capacity to solve those problems. Thus achieve the total development of a lamer.

### Role of teacher in curriculum development process

- Identification of need
- Formulation of Goals and Objectives
- Selection of Content
- Organization of Content
- Selection of Learning Experiences
- Organization of Learning Experiences
- Determination of what to evaluate and how to evaluate.

In short, the above discussion suggests that the curriculum is complex. The development of an effective curriculum is multi-step, continuous and cyclical process it involves different consideration of how policy transformed into practice. A successful curriculum reveals the success of a nation as whole, because the development of economy of a country depends the success of education sector. Therefore, the process of planning and implementing curriculum is complex in nature. The development of leaning and teaching resources will also need to change significantly to incorporate developments in digital platforms and broader access to online and digital resources in general.

## INNOVATIONS IN CURRICULUM DEVELOPMENT AND EVALUATION IN PRIMARY EDUCATION

Curriculum development is defined as a planned, purposeful, progressive, and systematic process to create positive improvements in the educational system. Every time there are changes or developments happening around the world. There is a need to update the school curricula to address the society's needs. Commonly used approaches in curriculum development consist of;

- *analysis*: need analysis and task analysis
- *design*: objective design

- *selecting*: choosing appropriate learning/teaching methods and appropriate assessment methods
- *formation*: formation of the curriculum implementation committee / curriculum evaluation committee and
- *review*: curriculum review committee

## Need for Innovations in the Curriculum

Innovations in the curriculum become inevitable with the change that takes place in a new and changing environment. Hence a number of specific factors are there to influence changes in the society. Some of the factors are as follows: explosion of knowledge, changes in society, social influences, changes in the organisational pattern of the school, development of new educational methods, National integration, values influencing change in curriculum, new experiments in child growth and development, explosion of population, selection of Curriculum materials, design of courses, National educational system, changes resulting from political and social pressures, changes arising from new subject content, changes arising from new concepts of management of the school, intellectual stirrings, community environment, computers and philosophical ideas. An innovation must fit in with the goals and objectives of education which usually reflect the needs, interests, values and problems of the society. It must be appropriate, economical in terms of time, space and resources and be aligned with the philosophy of the society and the school, and rooted in sound educational theory.

## Models of Curriculum Innovation

Various scholars have proposed different models of innovation. For instance, Ronald Havelock (1969) identified three main models of innovation: Research, Development, and Diffusion (RD&D) model, Social Interaction (SI) model, and Problem-Solving (PS) model.

- **The Research, Development and Diffusion (RD&D) Model:** In this model, an idea or practice is conceived at the central planning unit and then fed into the system. RD&D is effective where curriculum development is done on a large scale and ideas have to reach wide geographical areas and isolated users. It is a highly organised, rational approach to innovation.
- **The Social Interaction (SI) Model:** This model operates

through social interaction and emphasises communication. It stresses the importance of interpersonal networks of information, opinion of leadership, personal contacts, and social integration. The model also has its roots in the notion of democratic communities. The SI model also stresses the relationship of the individual to other people and society, and the instructional methods used by teachers in the classroom to facilitate group work. The model is student-centred, and students are encouraged to interact with each other in a structured setting. When implementing this strategy, students often serve as facilitators of content and help their peers to construct meaning. The students have to question, reflect, reconsider, seek help and support, and participate in group discussions. The three most common strategies include: group projects, group discussions, and cooperative learning (Patel, 2013).

- **The Problem Solving (PS) Model:** The PS model is based on the assumption that innovation is part of a problem-solving process. It is referred to as a "periphery-centre" approach to innovation. The innovations are initiated, generated, and applied by the teachers and schools based on their needs. Such innovations have strong user commitment and the best chance for long term survival. In this model, the receiver is actively involved in finding an innovation to solve their own unique problem. The model is flexible enough to encompass all types of innovations, including materials, methods, and groupings.

## Major trends in curriculum innovations

- A shift in educational goals and objectives towards using educational systems to prepare learners as functioning citizens of the 21st century.
- A move towards decentralising various aspects/ process of Curriculum development, implementation and administration.
- The national curriculum for basic education is being diversified precisely to meet the basic learning needs of different groups in the population.
- Emphasis on education programs that enhance science and Technology, literacy and are introducing as much ICT in schools as they can support.

- Emphasis on independent study or self-learning and of inculcating in students the love and desire to learn and the basic skills for learning.
- A shift from the traditional approaches where teachers are the major authority in knowledge transmission.
- Experimentation on various teaching learning methods and approaches to attain a better integration of the contents of the curriculum both within and across subject offerings.

## Paradigms in contemporary curriculum

- ***Joyful learning***: The term joyful learning in the context of education refers to the positive intellectual and emotional state of the learners. This state or experience is achieved when an individual or group derives pleasure and his sense of satisfaction from the process of learning.
- ***Experience learning:*** Experiential learning is also known as EXL. It is the process of learning through experience and is more specifically defined as learning through reflection on doing. Experiential learning is distinct from rote or didactic learning in which the learner plays a comparatively passive role.
- ***Guided learning:*** It is a term that refers to a process in which learners initiate and advance the learning guided by more experienced teachers, partners and socially derived sources such as tools, text and other artefacts. The exercise of learner agency is a defining quality of guided learning.

## Recommendations of National Educational Policy (NEP) 2020 on Primary Education

- There will be a 5+3+3+4 structure which comprises 12 years of school and 3 years of Anganwadi/ preschool replacing the old 10+2 structure.
- The new NEP is based on four pillars which are access, equity, quality and accountability.
- As per the vision of 2020 the government has approved the new India Literacy program (NILP) aiming at providing education for all, covering all aspects of education for non-literates of 15 years and above.

- Students now take a school examination which was conducted by the appropriate authority in grade 3, 5 and 8.
- Mathematical thinking and scientific temper coding will start from $6^{th}$ class.
- PARAKH (performance assessment, review and analysis of knowledge for Holistic development) a new National assessment platform will be developed for education. It will start in school from 6th grade which also includes internships.
- The new system will have 12 years of schooling and 3 years of Pre-school/Anganwadi till $5^{th}$ grade.
- This policy will emphasise local language/regional language/ mother tongue as the medium of instruction
- No student will be forced to speak any language through this policy. The children who are in the age of 3 to 6 years have access to free, safe, high quality, developmentally appropriate care and education by 2025.
- The new structure was designed in the interest of the learners at different stages of the development such as 3 to 8, 8 to 11,11 to 14 and 14 to 18 years.

## Innovations at International level

In international level coding and robotics are now implemented at the primary stage and is considered as a desirable change that helps students foster enhancement in creativity and logical thinking. Countries throughout the world are slowly and steadily adapting to various technological innovations. Educators are incorporating curriculums in school that focus on the all-round development of children. One such curriculum that has been widely accepted by schools around the world is the STEM curriculum. STEM stands for Science, Technology, Engineering and Mathematics. It focuses on the all-round development of students and helps students to develop critical thinking ability. Coding and Robotics are now implemented at the primary school level and is considered a desirable change that helps students foster enhancement in creativity and logical thinking. In short, primary education aims to lay the foundation for the development of children. Along with the academics, they teach students to grow and develop social skills, behaviour, personality, explore their interests and harness their creativity. Thus, one can say that a primary education provides an instrumental platform for the growth of children in all aspects of life ranging from academics to society and many more. Hence innovations in curriculum development are inevitable at primary level. Curriculum should be in harmony with the changing needs of the individual and the society.

## LEADERSHIP IN CURRICULUM

The word "curriculum" began as a Latin word which means "a race" or "the course of a race". From the historical perspective, curriculum is any document or plan of action that exists in a school or schools' system that defines the work of teachers. The term Curriculum refers to the lessons and academic content taught in a school or in a specific course or program. Creation of curriculum needs a great deal of thought, time, effort, and expertise. The success of a curriculum depends the sustainability and flexibility of its nature. A well-crafted Curriculum provides and serves a teacher to ensure that the teachers are in the right track. The modern, definition of curriculum is a plan tied to goals and related objectives. This definition suggests a process of choosing from among the many possible activities those that are preferred and, thus, value-laden. The curriculum is purposeful and defined. Activities shape student behaviours.

**Why curriculum is important?** A curriculum accomplishes these goals by: (1) Clarifying organizational boundaries, (2) Defining the nature of the work to be done, (3) Defining standards by which work is to be measured or assessed; (4) Defining evaluation procedures, (5) Making changes in the work performed through feedback; and (6) Measurement of work performance on a consistent basis.

### Leadership in curriculum

A curriculum leader is a person or a group of persons who have a vision, capacity to take many tasks associated with the curriculum development process and the leader is professionally responsible for sorting out and prioritizing this work. He also tries to build a team to work together over a period of time. A curriculum manager or leader would focus on reviewing materials, control issues, daily problem-solving, and encouraging a predictable routine from year to year. Effective curriculum leadership does all of those things plus establish new direction, align people and resources, motivate participants, and produce meaningful change for school improvement. In short, effective curriculum leadership is more than maintenance, it is dynamic in nature. The curriculum leaders must operate in an open, involving, and facilitating way to be successful. He contributes significant changes ever present and he always responding to change. Curriculum leadership means the effective modification and implementation of existing curriculum into a new one. Curriculum leader have a significant role in improving academic achievements. He always involved in the implementation of curriculum instruction, and assessment practices. The most important person in the curriculum implementation process is the teacher itself. With their knowledge, experiences and competencies, teachers are the central to curriculum development effort. Leadership in curriculum rest to the capacity to exercise functions that enable the achievement of learner's goals by providing quality education to the learners. All schools are not equal in achieving the desired improvements. It can be achieved through making maintenance of curriculum, so maintenance of curriculum is vital role in attainment of desired goals. If there is any balance between the maintaining the curriculum and upgrading school programs, the curriculum leader must always seek a greater and more visionary. The reason is that our world is not static and the curriculum in school represents our nation. So, the curriculum provides students to fulfil their future life.

## Curriculum Leadership Functions

- Develop the school's vision of quality curriculum.
- Develop the national or divisional educational goals.
- Develop the school's own program of studies.
- Develop a leaning centred schedule.
- Determine the nature and extent of curricula integration.
- Align the curriculum.
- Monitor and assist in curriculum implementation

## The challenges in practicing curriculum leadership

- Fast paced change imparting on the curriculum.
- Curriculum design that unresponsive to local needs.
- Lack of resource for proper implementation of curriculum content.

- Lack of organizational support.
- Lack of authority for exercise leadership role.

**Why schools need curriculum leaders. There are five reasons;**

- Curriculum Leadership provides clarity
- Curriculum Leadership provides opportunities to develop and empower future leaders.
- Curriculum Leadership provides the opportunity for continuous improvement.
- Curriculum Leadership provides the opportunity to establish goals.
- Curriculum Leadership provides the opportunity for improved alignment.

**Role of Curriculum Leaders**

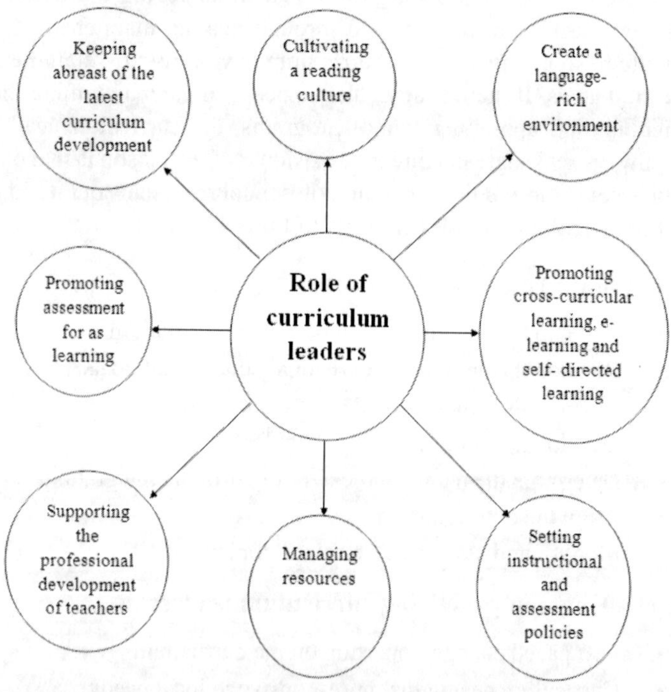


*Figure 3.1: Role of curriculum leaders*

## Dynamic Curriculum Leader

Dynamic curriculum leader is a person he moves the faculty and the community beyond the minimum standards and toward clear and larger goals for the students by using any intellectual transition. He must focus attention on how to organize the content of curriculum to meet the needs of learners and individualizing instruction, because the learners are not alike and they have different strengths and intelligences. The world view of the curriculum leader is dynamic in nature. Dynamic curriculum leadership will require planning in the areas like, whole nation's plan of change, others contribution to school improvement, etc. A dynamic curriculum leader always seeks to move from where are the present to an improved condition for our students and the organization. The dynamic view of a curriculum leader is that an active process involving the continual construction and improvement of school programs periodically. A dynamic leader can change the learners and organization as whole dynamic.

## Difference between Leadership in curriculum and management in curriculum

| Leadership in curriculum | Management in curriculum |
|---|---|
| Requires questioning the current enterprise of curriculum writing and creating something that is far more effective. | Is fundamentally concerned with effective teaching and learning. |
| Requires a new vision | It is easy to grasp |
| Curriculum leadership involves a careful balance of instructional and administrative leadership responsibilities. | Find solutions to deal with all tasks related to brainstorming, developing, integrating, and launching curriculum |
| Leaders must ensure that targets for improvement in the Curriculum | It consists of managing what students are expected to learn, evaluating whether or not it was learned, and seeking ways to improve student learning. |

Finally, the curriculum leader who is dynamic will need to understand the many needs of the institution and the resources that exist to boost change efforts and empower the curriculum development process in schools. The skilful use of committees, technologies, assessments, and other tools will contribute to a successful attainment of group goals. Comprehensive planning, design, and modernization of schools and the direction of career technical education and how it will bring a renewing obsolete curriculum and inspire students to become self-motivated and equipped for the twenty first century high tech job market. The role of a curriculum leader is complex in nature because he satisfies the needs of both learners and the institution as a whole.

## INNOVATIONS IN EVALUATION IN PRIMARY EDUCATION

"Evaluation is a continuous process aimed at helping the student to improve his level of achievement rather than at certifying the quality of his performance at a given moment of time" - National Policy on Education (1969). School evaluation is an important part of quality education. In essence, evaluation is feedback for the evaluated individual on the quality of their performance, results and efficiency of their performed work, but it also contributes to the development of the personality of the pupil and their self-evaluation ability, which can be applied throughout their future life

### Types of Evaluation

**Summative Evaluation:** Summative evaluation or assessment of learning is the assessment of participants where the focus is on the outcome of a program and the evaluation will be done at the end of the programme or in the middle of the programme. Summative evaluation, sometimes called a final evaluation, has the ultimate meaning to get a final overall view of a pupil's performance. It establishes the level of knowledge gained over a period of time and for example admission tests can be a typical example. Unlike formative evaluation, a summative evaluation doesn't address pupil performance over time but only the final statement. Pupil motivation is more external than internal. This type of evaluation isn't as effective as formative evaluation but it's also very important for personality development and informative function. Often this evaluation is only based on the average of all pupils' marks over a certain period of time - for example, half-yearly. Thoughtful formative evaluation should be added to the average of the marks so that pupil's approach worse marks positively and their motivation continues to develop for further performance. This evaluation is often stressful for pupils and they may feel limited by the evaluation scale. E.g.: End-of-term or midterm exams.

**Normative Evaluation**: Normative evaluation is a type of relative performance evaluation, where the benchmark is the very important criterion in which we perform this evaluation. The measure is a social norm established with respect to a particular pupil group or population.

**Formative Evaluation:** It is also called continuous evaluation and it's already evident that it's focused on the ongoing evaluation of pupils' educational progress. It allows pupils to have time for substance acquisition and follow-up learning. Feedback from teachers and pupils plays an important role. Through teachers' feedback, pupils have an overview of their progress and lessons focused on their future performance. Teachers provide information that they can follow to meet a pupil's needs. This evaluation is based on a pupil's active participation in them learning process and the development of their "learn to learn" abilities. Formative evaluation is the first step on the way to the pupil's autonomous evaluation so that the pupil can learn and later they can recognise for themselves what is good in their work, what to develop and what to improve. E.g. Continuous and Comprehensive Evaluation (CCE).

## Innovative Formative Assessment Practices

- **Concept Map** – Concept maps are excellent tools of evaluating student learning and misunderstanding after the students were exposed to a new topic. In this a concept map will be prepared by the instructor with blank spaces and the students were asked to complete it.
- **Self-assessment** - Self-assessment is a way of encouraging children to evaluate and assess their own learning. Here, asking students to grade their own performance and pupils give feedback to themselves.
- **Peer assessment** - Peer assessment enables children to give each other valuable feedback so they learn from and support each other. It adds so much more to learning and the opportunity to talk, discuss, explain and challenge enables children to often achieve more than they would unaided.
- **Inquiry based evaluation** - Assessment of inquiry learning involves giving a value to student work related to the curriculum expectations at a given point in time - both at end

of each stage and at the end of inquiry- and then assigning a grade.

- **Role plays -** Role play exercises give students the opportunity to assume the role of a person or act out a given situation. These roles can be performed by individual students, in pairs, or in groups which can play out a more complex scenario.
- **Short, Regular, Quizzes -** A great deal of information can be learned from students by conducting quizzes regularly but it should be short, not much time consuming.
- **Round Robin** - The "Round robin" option is a technique for generating and developing ideas in a group brainstorming setting. It relies on an interactive process building off consecutive contributions by each participant, conducted in either written or verbal variations. This strategy may also involves passing charts among groups to assess understanding
- **Strategic Questioning** - Questioning strategies may be used with individuals, small groups, or the entire class.
- **Way Summaries** - In response to a question or topic inquiry, they write three different summaries: 10–15 words long, 30–50 words long, 75–100 words long.
- **Think-Pair-Share** – Here the instructor asks a question, and students write down their answers. Students are then placed in pairs to discuss their responses. Teachers are able to move around the classroom and listen to various discussions.
- **3–2–1 Countdown** - They are required to respond to three separate statements: three things you didn't know before, two things that surprised you about this topic, one thing you want to start doing with what you've learned
- **Classroom Polls** – It allows instructors to quickly ask a question and instantly receive responses from student s during the class
- **Exit/Admit Tickets** - Exit tickets are small pieces of paper or cards that students deposit as they leave the classroom. Students write down an accurate interpretation of the main idea behind the lesson taught that day. Admit tickets are done at the very beginning of the class. Students may

respond to questions about homework, or on the lesson taught the day before.

- **Group Projects** – Project-based assessments are an alternative to tests that allow students to engage with their learning in more concrete ways. Instead of merely studying theory, a hands-on project asks students to apply what they've learned to an in-depth exploration of a topic. Working in student groups to complete a project, will give a clear idea about the social skill and compatibility of students.
- **Portfolio -** A student portfolio is a compilation of academic work and other forms of educational evidence assembled for the purpose of evaluating coursework quality, learning progress, and academic achievement; determining whether students have met learning standards or other academic requirements for courses, grade-level.

## Innovative evaluation strategies proposed by NEP 2020

- Formative evaluation
- Self-evaluation
- Peer evaluation
- Project based assessment
- Evaluation in enquiry-based learning
- Quizzes
- Role plays
- Group work
- Holistic progress reports

In short, Evaluation is an important component of the teaching-learning process. It helps teachers and learners to improve teaching and learning. Evaluation is a continuous process not a periodic exercise. It helps in forming the values of judgement, educational status, or achievement of students. Evaluation provides a systematic method to study a program, practice, intervention, or initiative to understand how well it achieves its goals. Evaluations help to determine what works well and what could be improved in a program or initiative. Thus, it is essential that there should be proper assessment practices in primary schools. It helps to identify students' strengths and weaknesses and the gaps they may have in their learning/skills. It also assists in setting targets for students/grades/subject specializations. It helps to review and monitor teaching and learning strategies and process. It also encourages reflection and introspection about learning.

## REFERENCES

1. Admin (2021). *List of Education Commissions in India*, https://learnitspro.com/list-of-education-commissions-in-india-pdf/
2. Agarwal, Y. *Quality Concerns in Primary Education in India: Where is the Problem*, NIEPA New Delhi
3. Aggarwal, J. C. (1990). *Curriculum Reforms in India: World Overview.* Doaba House, Delhi.
4. Ayyar,V.R.V. (2016).*The Holy Grail: India's Quest for Universal Elementary Education*, New Delhi: Oxford University Press.
5. Biswas, A., and Agrawal, S.P. (1986). *Development of Education in India: A Historical Survey of Educational Documents Before and After Independence*. Concept Publishing Company.
6. CBSE. (2011). *Continuous and Comprehensive Evaluation*, http://cbse.nic.in/cce/index.html#
7. *Committees and Commissions for the Development of Teacher Education during Post-Independent India: A Review*, VOCEDplus, the International Tertiary Education and Research Database, https://www.voced.edu.au/content/ngv%3A2144 (February 16, 2022).
8. Dayaram (2002). *Para Teachers in Primary Education – A Status Report*, DPEP
9. Development of Education in India after Independence (2014). *Economics Discussion.* https://www.economicsdiscussion.net/articles/development-of-education-in-india-after-independence/2293 (February 16, 2022).
10. Dholakia, R.H. & Iyengar, S. (2008). *Access of Poor Households to Primary Education in Rural India*, www.iimahd.ernet.in/publications/data/2008-02-02RDholakia.pdf
11. *Education - The Postindependence Period in India*, https://www.britannica.com/topic/education/The-postindependence-period-in-India (February 16, 2022).
12. *Educational Committees and Commissions*, https://taleemiboard.org/wp-content/uploads/2020/02/Educational-Committees-and-Commissions.pdf (February 16, 2022).
13. *Goals and Governance of Higher Education in India,* https://link.springer.com/article/10.1007/s10734-012-9565-9 (February 16, 2022).
14. https://egov.uok.edu.in/courseinfo/syllabus/syllabusArchive/2118.PDF

15. https://teachingtools.ophea.net/supplements/inquiry-based-learning/assessment-inquiry-based-learning

16. https://www.jstor.org/stable/44417291

17. https://www.researchgate.net/publication/314281465_Project_based_learning_in_the_primary_school_classroom

18. https://www.researchgate.net/publication/329939782_Types_and_Forms_of_Evaluation_at_Primary_School_from_the_Viewpoint_of_Teachers

19. https://www.scholarify.in/innovations-in-evaluation-systems

20. https://www.schoology.com/blog/how-students-benefit-project-based-assessments-examples

21. https://www.teachprimary.com/learning_resources/view/using-peer-assessment-in-the-primary-classroom

22. Krishnamacharyulu, V., & Ramarao, V.P. (2012). *Elementary Education.* Neelkamal Publications Pvt. Ltd., Hyderabad.

23. *Leading Curriculum Innovation in Primary Schools.* (2004, January 1). Research gate, https://www.researchgate.net/publication/228954550_

24. Ministry of Human Resource Development, Dept. School Education and Literacy, India. (2017). Right to Education Act, Controller of Publication, Delhi.

25. NCERT (1971) *Education and National Development: Report of the Education Commission 1964-66*

26. Premji, A. (Feb 19, 2008). *India Growth Story Needs Good Quality Education*, Published in Economics Times

27. Premji, A. (Nov 16, 2003): *Improve Access, Quality of Education*, published in India Times; New Delhi, infotech.indiatimes.com/.../Improve... quality...education.../286526.cms

28. Rajni (2021). *Historical Background of Primary Education in India: At a Glance.* Shodh Sarita.

29. *Redefining innovation in education for primary school kids.* (2020, October 21). Times of India. https://timesofindia.indiatimes.com/readersblog/lifecrunch/redefining-innovation-in-education-for-primary-school-kids-27374/

30. SCERT. (2007). *Kerala Curriculum Framework.* Thiruvananthapuram: SCERT

31. Sharma, S. (2002). *History and Development of Higher Education in India.* Sarup & Sons.

32. Stephens, D. (2003). *Quality of Basic Education, International Journal of Educational Primary Education*, unesdoc.unesco.org/images/001469/146968e.pdf

33. The Constitution (86th Amendment) Act. (2002). Govt. of India.

34. Varghese, N.V., & Garima, M. (2015). *India Higher Education Report 2015*. Routledge.

35. Wight, D., & Pradnyasurya, S. (2018). *A Critical Analysis of National & State Commissions and Committees of De-notified, Nomadic and Semi-Nomadic Tribes in India*